STANISLAVSKI'S FOURTH LEVEL
A Superconscious Approach to Acting

STANISLAVSKI'S FOURTH LEVEL

A Superconscious Approach to Acting

Ned Manderino

MANDERINO BOOKS
Los Angeles
WWW.MANDERINO.COM

STANISLAVSKI'S FOURTH LEVEL:
A Superconscious Approach to Acting

For information contact:
  Manderino Books
  P.O. Box 27758
  Los Angeles, CA 90027
or ned@manderino.com
  www.manderino.com

ISBN: 0-9601194-8-5
Library of Congress Control Number: 2001129196

Manuscript Publication Design:
Angel Pages, Los Angeles, CA

Printed by McNaughton & Gunn, Saline MI
Graphic Design by Rick Herold
Cover Layout by three-sixty graphics

First printing, 2001.

ACKNOWLEDGMENTS

The author wishes to express his gratitude to Anita Colby for her invaluable editorial assistance for this publication and three previous publications.

The author also feels much indebted to Richard Silver, a superb actor who, "acting" as Aristotle to my Plato, imparted vital additional editing with sensitivity and remarkable wisdom.

Thanks are also extended to Jason DeAngelis, a highly versatile actor in the author's ongoing workshop, for his careful reading of the galleys.

This book is dedicated to the memory of Edwin "Chip" DuBose whose heroic nature led him to save the lives of three strangers in danger of drowning at sea, relinquishing his first place lead in a prestigious boat race.

"We have so little time on this earth and we should do the best we can."

Ethel Kennedy

CONTENTS

Author's Note

The superconscious exercises in this book represent a higher level of acting study. Although it is possible that a talent can benefit from the exercises in this book with little or no training or experience—certainly some actors have become successful with little or no training or experience—I strongly feel that most actors will experience maximum gain from the book following a period of basic sensory technique training. I have guided numerous actors through the high-creative superconscious exercises in this book, but I have never done so without an actor having a preliminary preparation in the basic Stanislavski philosophy.

If you have had sensory training, this book will hopefully challenge you beyond your present range. Choices from your sensory training can be effectively combined with any of the exercises in this book.

For readers who wish to have an extensive knowledge of basic Method sensory exercises, may I refer you to All About Method Acting, a book I have authored that guides my workshop actors through their initial phase of training before entering into an advanced adventure with the superconscious exercises.

What else do I suggest is required of you? Well, Stanislavski was convinced that an actor's imagination must be a powerful, utilized force. The exercises herein will require the best use of your imagination.

As you read this book, the exercises may initially seem unusual and unconventional, perhaps even unrelated to reality. If this brings about any hesitancy, I urge you to keep in mind, that within the context of acting artistry, truthful realities of story elements, such as characterization, plot and theme, can be conveyed through the proper use of "unreal" or imagined energies.

Therefore, when approaching the superconscious exercises, give your imagination free reign with the realization that anything that the human body can imagine and experience is nourishment for the expression of behavioral choices and theatrical realities. Imagination is regarded as the source of our creativity and as our most outstanding possession which has led us, from the beginning, to the success we enjoy as humans on this planet.

As you probe and absorb this book's essence, I believe you will inevitably experience transformations in your acting technique. Using your seemingly endless creative reserves to power your imagination is all you will need to experience superconsciousness in your talent, enabling your acting instrument to unleash superconscious energies and soar.

Part I

Introduction to the Technique Exercises

Part I:
Introduction to the Technique Exercises

THE FOURTH LEVEL:
Realm of the Superconscious

While resting in a sanitarium near Moscow in 1935, several years before his death, Stanislavski told a group of visitors that thoroughly trained actors can forget their technique training and abandon themselves to what he described as the fourth floor of consciousness. (This book takes the liberty to change the word "floor", originally translated from Stanislavski's writings in Russian, to the word "level" for its contemporary sensibility and effectiveness.)

This book offers a technique method to guide you towards Stanislavski's fourth level and to strengthen within you the creative consciousness needed to occupy it. The inclusion of technique exercises in this book are intended to help you experience the strong behavioral results which countless actors have created and productively incorporated into their techniques. The exercises in this book go beyond the basic sensory exercises developed in America during the 1920s and 1930s which granted power to an actor's innate sense of truth. However, we no longer live in the comparatively static world of that time which was congenial to the use of sensory exercises. A cyclical succession of shocking and horrific events around the world, and now, even within our own country, has changed everything.

Sensory awareness in the human experience has now given way to an expansion of the consciousness. Consciousness awareness exercises enable the individual to make contact with the higher creative energy centers of the psyche. Stanislavski coined the word *"superconscious"* to allude to the state that an actor should strive towards and implied that actors studying his System without expanding it would not be able to find its full potency. His autobiography, more than his popular technique books, has many references to the spiritual in acting. By spiritual, Stanislavski did not necessarily imply matters of a theological nature. Instead, his concept of the spiritual implied the growth and fulfillment of an individual's given potential which, as we are well aware, is of paramount concern as we move into the third millennium.

It took years of experimentation for Stanislavski to formulate his system. He had a number of failures and was ridiculed by his contemporaries. Once he found his path, though, he functioned as if no other ideas about acting existed. He searched everywhere to develop his System. He watched great actors and questioned them about their technique, observed his own acting, and studied Hindu philosophy and yoga. His first book, *An Actor Prepares,* was thirty five years in preparation and was not published until he was 73. He never stopped growing and exploring, and as a result his later books often contradict his first. At the end of his life, he felt that he was at the beginning of his search.

Stanislavski had a strong belief in innovation. He believed that a person can benefit from studying the work of a predecessor and then improving upon it. Though "innovation" has become a newly popularized term in contemporary entrepreneurship, it has been a part of evolution of any art since the beginning of time. Innovations stem from the human impulse to improve upon what has come before. All innovation is destructive of the past—of old ways of seeing, doing, creating. The course of history offers innumerable examples of one generation improving upon the ideas, knowledge, and techniques of the previous generation.

In working with actors, my intention has always been to elevate their acting instruments to a higher level and enrich their imaginations by having them select choices beyond traditional Method acting choices and enter the realm of the superconsciousness.

Solid technique training is required for most actors to rise, even approximately, to the level of genius talents. Every young actor wants to be as good as great actors are and is curious to know what is going on inside their artistic psyche and persona that creates the chemistry of their greatness. It was the search for the chemistry of genius technique that originally impelled Stanislavski towards the development of his System. He sought to approximate in his acting what he believed genius actors had in common, particularly the ability to create strong emotions that possessed fully loaded physicality and an inner core of truth, logic and imagination.

As an actor, you pass through different states of conscious awareness during your development. In moving forward, you experience the force of a new creative truth, and if the reality of it feels right, you naturally adopt it as your own. Part of your psyche benefits from cultivating higher states of peak experiences. Many actors regard each new state as an epiphany leading to a transcendence. Stanislavski referred to the bodily form and substance of a peak acting experience as the "incarnation of a role." The important element is that you be able to evaluate what has happened. The description and explanation of exercises in this book give you the means to define what has occurred in each exercise so that you need not be uncertain or puzzled by it.

Stanislavski spoke many times of the actor's future resting on inspirational intuition. He believed that the actor's instrument should be trained in such a way that the mechanics of technique need not be dwelled upon and that an actor be able to perform with virtuoso effortlessness. I do believe that he would agree with the contemporary concept of intuition as being a phenomenon that occurs instantaneously, surfacing magnificently as it seemingly bypasses the usual creative channels in an actor's instrument, but in actuality, results from their full integration. The exercises in this book are intended to help you arrive at a stronger state of creative intuition, regardless of the juncture your career presently occupies.

INTUITION AND
THE FOURTH LEVEL

Once having honed and internalized a technique, the actor is capable of transcending it,
rendering the art of acting effortless and spontaneous which are traits of the intuitive process.
For the actor who has stored-up an arsenal of
technique choices, creative solutions surface with
ease from the subliminal integration of technique
knowledge. This experience is often described as
a transcendent one and occurs only during a truly
committed career journey toward the total mas-
tery of one's craft. It arrives with the sudden force
of a peal of thunder and signifies a new aesthetic
and an enhanced acting power. Years of developing one's craft are rewarded when all at once, the
actor has both the capacity and the courage to
inhabit a role with complete trust in the creative
impulses that are part of one's birthright. The
actor is suddenly released from a reliance on
technique principles and can function through
intuition. This revelatory moment has been described variously as letting things happen ... enlightenment ... beyond craft ... beyond the barriers of traditional aesthetics ... no approach ...
above technique ... the zone of indifference ...
and being at one with oneself. Each of these descriptions reflects the individual's sense of having reached a destination or completed a cycle.
Bidding adieu to the conscious employment of
technique, the actor is able to hit the target effortlessly, like a Zen archer. Technique has been
so deeply absorbed into the heart, mind and soul

of the actor that it now flows effortlessly—without serving as a tangible conduit between the actor and the role.

Performance intuition permits the actor to open up the floodgates of the acting instrument to allow the free flow of talent. Letting one's talent flow requires courage and confidence. A prerequisite of performance intuition is a systematically trained and disciplined instrument. Limited or narrow training sets you on the beginning of a path but leaves you stranded creatively. At best such training affords you a shallow naturalism. Unfortunately, many suffer from a delusion that the Muses have blessed them and they therefore require only limited training.

A professional musician practices scales for years in order to reach those second-nature performance levels that seem so effortless in concert. Musicians continue to practice scales throughout their careers, just as singers continue to vocalize their scales and ballet dancers continue to spend hours each day at the bar practicing basic steps. Similarly, an actor who has achieved performance intuition cannot rest on victorious laurels, but rather, must provide constant nourishment for the continued growth and development of the acting instrument. The artistic journey never ends; it leads instead to unforeseeable adventures, new and more stimulating challenges and endless possibilities.

Performance intuition taps into a reservoir of marshaled resources including:

- Your imagination and originality
- Your natural harmony
- Your intelligence
- Your knowledge of craft
- Your creative vitality and flair
- The fluidity of your acting instrument
- The richness of your vocal qualities
- Your plasticity
- Your physical grace and presence
- Your courage and boldness
- Your sense of security vs. your sense of adventure
- Your psychological insight
- Your drive to excel and go beyond your limits
- The infectiousness of your emotional state
- Your willingness to take risks
- Your thirst for knowledge
- Your charm, humility, honesty, and integrity
- Your perfectionism

Using these resources, you will intuitively know whether an interpretation is on course or not.

Certainly, there will be occasions when you suddenly feel stuck and call upon the golden keys you discovered while your were developing your technique. No one is immune from the incursion of uncertainty, and it is enormously reassuring that the keys are still embedded in your acting instrument, ready to come forth on a conscious level when you need them. Sometimes, you may exercise your technique skills simply to assure yourself that they are still there.

Even though the achievement of performance intuition represents a true pinnacle, the pursuit of one's art is never truly completed. But isn't that what the life of a creative actor is all about?

METHOD ACTING AT A GLANCE

Following is a brief overview of some of the Method acting principles that are mentioned in this book. For anyone who is only vaguely familiar with Method acting, it offers an explanation of technique terms. If you are already acquainted with them, this section will allow you to confirm your present Method acting techniques and, perhaps, refresh them.

ABOUT METHOD ACTING

The appeal of Method acting stems from its ability to inspire greater individuality in an acting talent. Method technique has gained an international reputation for creating behavior in a dynamic and naturalistic way. The Method requires that the actor give less emphasis to an "outer" interpretation (encompassing vocal and physical qualities) of the character's words, focusing instead on giving clarity to a character's intentions through an "inner" interpretation (encompassing thoughts, emotions and sensations). Through the use of "actions" and the development of a more acute sensory awareness, the experience of a character is internalized, and, simultaneously, elements are created which acknowledge the necessity of outer characterization.

As the Method has been applied in America, innumerable controversies have arisen about the "true" interpretation of Stanislavski principles. Representatives of the differing schools have accused each other of distorting and misinterpreting the Method, viewing each other as malpractitioners of the system. The central point of the furor concerns the belief that some who teach or practice the Method overemphasize the creation of truthful inner emotion without giving attention to the important outer aspects needed to create a character in a dramatic situation. Many people feel that the Method is misused when the actor works with personal emotional experience in a way that neglects the outer essence of the character. In other words, they would argue that the character's theatrical truth should not be given short shrift by the choices the Method actor uses to create personal emotion. My own point of view is that the truly creative actor gives attention to both the inner and outer of a character's existence. In other words, creative acting is a synthesis of both the inner and outer.

The examples of actions and choices at the end of each chapter were chosen by actors I have coached. They are included to arouse your imagination in the selection of your own actions and choices as you practice the exercises. Actions, for those of you not acquainted with the term, refer not only to physical behavior of a character; the rich meaning of actions also encompasses the inner thoughts, emotions and feelings of the character. (Actions are also called or referred to as intentions, objectives or motivations.) The conscious use of actions enables the actor to have pinpoint clarity about the character's intentions. Identifying a character's actions enables the actor to plan the human behavior of a character, basing it on a precise knowledge of what the character is wishing, wanting and willing at any given moment. Many of the actions listed in the appendix are not the straightforward, one-verb actions that are commonly used. In my experience, many actors prefer actions stated as "juiced up" phrases which stimulate their imagination to a greater degree.

Actions dictate the number of sections in a role. You analyze and break down a script into sections by first determining the actions. Some actions will span a line or a few lines of script while others can be quite lengthy. Actions are not to be dealt with in an arbitrary way; instead, each change of action must be fully justified. An action for any given section remains the same as long as the lines are applicable to the action. When the lines are no longer applicable, a new section begins and a new action arises. A sections ends because the action has been fulfilled or not fulfilled. In either case, a new action is needed. With film scripts, each shot does not dictate a change of action. If the lines are applicable, an action can cover a series of shots. In film acting, the action is a lifeline; it affords the actor the control and concentration needed to deal with the technical disruptions of filmmaking. By determining a character's actions, you can perform the role completely out of sequence which is often required by production schedules. As long as you are aware of the action of each shot, you can avoid vagueness about the role, even if the shots are broken up over several days. Your firm grasp of actions would certainly be a boon in situations where retakes are done months later. A list of actions can be found in the appendix of this book beginning on page 171. Selecting an action when practicing the exercises will help you to form a "story" during your practice time. They can also be used to interpret monologues and scenes.

THE SENSES

The senses are your tools as much as your voice, speech and physical self. The senses can be harnessed and strengthened to create truthful realities. Sense memory stirs the creative subconscious. The sense organs are the organs of concentration in Method acting since it is through them that organic and spontaneous behavior results. Sense memory teaches you how to create the physical, as well as the inner life of a character. Since your main concern is searching for behavior, sense memory training serves a definite purpose. Through the retraining and greater awareness of the senses, your individuality is sharpened. Creative use of the senses can also induce behavior and colors that are not part of your personality. Sense memory exercises can also be a powerful catalyst in dissolving ingrained mannerisms so that fresh expressiveness can occur.

Work with sense memory employs creative exercises that call upon the five senses of sight, sound, taste, touch and smell. Highly talented actors have described how creative sensory exercises enabled them to refine their acting instruments, and attest to the value such exercises have in keeping the instrument in tune. Pianists, dancers and singers devote many hours of the day to their creative talents, even when the talent is working well. The amount of time you spend depends on the extent you wish to perfect a talent and keep it in shape—and this applies both to sensory exercise practice and to the practice of superconscious exercises in this book (which are a form of advanced sensorial experience).

CHOICES

In this book, you will find examples of an action listed along with one or more technique exercises. The exercise or exercises you select are referred to as a "choice" or "choices." The choice(s) will lead you to evoke emotions and behavior related to the action. The aforementioned lists of actions and choices are those actually selected and effectively used by actors I have coached in my workshop.

An actor with a great sense of freedom will invariably have an enormous amount of choices at his or her disposal. With this bounty of riches will come the task of having to decide which to use. In researching a role, one might amass a large arsenal of choices to select from and thus, find it necessary to whittle them down to only those which are particularly affecting. Shakespeare, for example, surely had many possibilities for shaping any particular line of dialogue, but always chose what he considered to be the best.

For many Method actors, sensory choices are ingrained in their technique. Their choices feed the imagination and, if properly done, enable them to avoid acting clichés. What gives the use of a choice its appealing spontaneity are the unplanned results. You do not strive for planned results but become involved with the choice at the moment it is being created. This gives the moment the quality of behavior happening for the first time.

You can have a multitude of ideas that keep burbling up in the mind; choices provide the means of making them specific. At times, you will employ many choices in order to instill a moment with different dimensions of a character's personality. Some well-known actors have said that they prefer to employ choices in this way because it gives "flash" and "flamboyance" to their vision and creation of a character. The simultaneous use of several choices reflects the synergies, complexities and contradictory elements in human behavior. At other times, you will discover that a more focused concentration, using fewer choices, will be preferable.

INNER DETAIL/OUTER DETAIL

The exercises in this book, as with any of the sensory exercises, relate to both inner and outer behavior in acting.

Actors sometimes explain their approach to a role as starting from the outside (often overdoing the resulting outer behavior) and then gradually going inside for final exploration. There are also actors who use a reverse approach, exploring the inner detail before adding the outer, or the "overcoat," as it is sometimes called. Still, a third group will work on both simultaneously, as inner exploration gives immediate rise to outer details (and vice versa).

The strengthening of the inner state of the actor is emphasized by most acting teachers, while concern with visceral and vocal power are proffered by others; both approaches are of value. Too much concern with the inner process can be detrimental and result in what has been called bottled-up emotions.

The inner and outer process is perhaps more noticeable in the creation of a stage play, which can be a long, drawn out process compared to working in a film which is concerned only with the results needed from a day's shooting. In the rehearsal of a stage play, procedures will vary. However, good actors and good directors are aware that although everyone might be working differently, they are still all effused with the spirit of reaching the goal of an ensemble performance.

Top actors admit that if their jobs depended on what they revealed during early rehearsals, they would be replaced, and that it is only the director's awareness of their process that enables them to keep their jobs. Some actors undertake their roles with a certain flashiness, boldly letting out spontaneous images in a bravura manner, at first, and then beginning the sensitive selection of values and colors as they move toward internalized meanings. Other actors completely conceal what they are doing, and only when ready, will they permit inner conceptions to surface. In those actors, it is as if the nature of outer detail miraculously grew from the roots of inner detail.

LEVELS OF TECHNIQUE

> *There are as many different acting techniques as there are actors—just as in Tibet there are as many different Buddhist sects as there are lamas.*

Technique grows from the gradual accumulation of great volumes of knowledge and enables you to skillfully execute the dramatic intentions of any role. This arsenal of information prevents you from repetitive self-indulgence, forced emotion and lack of credibility. When technique is skillfully and artistically embedded in your acting instrument, you can be assured that it will serve you dutifully and permit you a strong grip on creative details. We all have the inalienable right to change our minds about the technique beliefs we have fostered—you, as you extend your range of technique consciousness with this book, and I, by streamlining previously propounded technique principles in order to offer you the fullest development of my research.

When I began to teach, I quickly reinterpreted my understanding of viable acting techniques without feeling that I abdicated anything I had learned from the best of my teachers. I simply realigned their beliefs with my conviction that the entire problem with the use of the Stanislavski System is that it has failed to draw out hidden energies. As I stated earlier, Stanislavski himself implied that actors studying his System without expanding its energy would not be able to find its full potency.

As has been the case with each of my previous publications, my ongoing research has led me to new convictions and new insights. As our consciousness levels keep rising with new dynamics, theories and practices in all fields of human endeavor, beliefs that may have once had meaning become altered and, in some instances, may have less importance, and sometimes even cease to be useful.

A trained actor, contented with previous instruction, might be reluctant to give up a honed and comfortable technique (particularly if it leads to being offered work) for an "untried" technique. A beginning actor, on the other hand, possessing a more contemporary sensibility, might be inclined to add higher consciousness to the study of long-established paths of acting technique. The wise among beginning and developing actors are more experimental and adaptive because they have no desire to go through a training period, nor an entire career for that matter, without striving for and realizing their creative heights. They recognize those heights might be made reachable through new approaches of technique.

This book will permit you to define how the experience of a technique happened and give you a sense of how you "charged your batteries" to make it happen and the technique skill to repeat it when desired. You will never 'confuse yourself' or 'confront yourself' with questions such as "Where did that come from?" or "How did I create that experience?"

Actors who are dissatisfied with being regarded as types, or believe that they have become rusty because of a dry spell in acquiring work, have been known to be open to new ways of using their talents. Oftentimes, great talents are intrigued by exploring new artistic vistas. Consider the great dancer Margot Fonteyn who, at the height of a glorious career, welcomed the risks and challenges that a new, youthful partner, Rudolf Nureyev, gave to her dancing. In the process, she prolonged her career past the time when her retirement was expected by some in the dance world.

Artists have always been intrigued by the innovative elements and new ways of creative expression that are inevitably experienced during high states of awareness when a vision or insight can trigger an enormous amount of something unusual and new. History reflects this in the accomplishments of artists—and also those of astronomers, philosophers, mathematicians and scientists.

As actors pass through stages of development and growth, they can, to various degrees, "jump around" from one technique to another. This "jumping around" is one part of the artistic search for new knowledge and the actor's renaissance journey towards the edge of perfection.

Ultimately, you discover that as you go from one technique to another it is still technique, but with a different name. In the process put forward in this book, you are not asked or required to totally dissolve your present *technique identity*. You may, nevertheless, discover that what you are artistically doing has grown stale and mundane. The exercises are intended to enrich your present identity and, for some of you, can be useful for a reinvention of self. You may have already engaged in this process one or more times when asking yourself: "Am I comfortable with the image I present? Do I need to refine it or even change it? Do I dare abandon my present technique beliefs? Is it possible that by stepping into unknown territory, I might undergo a useful transformation?"

These questions will help you to find out how you can bend what you already know to something closer to your imagination. Many actors find themselves needing a change of image at some point in their careers. An actor's image might be tarnished by the wrong roles, personal misconduct, disastrous miscasting or dark rumors. The shady limelight of titillating gossip and stigmatizing tabloids often mandates an image change. An image change is definitely required for actors who have a reputation for being difficult in their work and public relationships. Their close associates are behooved to sit down with them and point out the necessity for steering a course of amity.

Before beginning to sculpt a more engaging image, you need to examine the nature of your existing image. Your desired image will take creative form only if you have an explicit idea of the qualities you wish to foster and nourish. Picasso said that a painter "walks around for months with a movie of images in his mind and he winds up with one image." Artists in varied media can be obsessed with an image or an idea, which will inhabit their waking and sleeping hours, persisting until it is finally consummated. When you have begun to visualize the new image you wish to cultivate, the vision will likewise stay with you until the image has fully flowered. To bring the image to full fruition, you must pump blood into it, creating a living, believable, comfortable image. The process is not unlike the way one penetrates into the heart and soul of a role.

A new image should be molded with a sense of high craftsmanship. Changing your image should not be a whim or passing fancy. It is a process of artistic transformation, not a process of tinkering with a not-quite-tuned image. The transformation must not seem calculated, assaulting, overly indulgent, ostentatious, nor inelegant. Any of these traits can have negative repercussions among decision-makers. Neither casting agents, directors, nor audiences are particularly drawn toward a self-conscious image.

Acting styles vary from one decade to the next, and it is the insightful actor who captures them until something new comes along, as it inevitably does.

Many mid-career actors engage in one of many types of workshops to reexamine the effectiveness of their instruments' qualities. Workshops also serve to establish the degree to which qualities have ripened, the desirability of further refinement, or even the need for a complete image overhaul. As a distinct new image takes final shape, it becomes a springboard for roles which are opposite to that of previous roles. The maturation of a new image can give birth to a more successful career and perhaps vest you with the privilege of choosing and rejecting roles.

It requires a rebel spirit to evolve into a new state of awareness if you believe that your technique theory has not evolved. With this book, you will encounter truths that will lead you to a more highly creative use of your talent. It will require of you to go beyond what you ever expected, perfecting and enhancing what is already working for you. That can be an enormously gratifying experience as you become aware of transformative technique skills.

SUPERCONSCIOUSNESS AND SPIRITUALITY

Einstein said that mystical emotion is not only beautiful but it is also "the doer of all art and science."

Routes for leaping into realms of sensory awareness and superconsciousness have gained wide popularity via myriad self-help books, among which, if you wish, you can include this book. Bookstores are well stocked with tomes reflecting a vast number of disciplines, spiritual beliefs and growth guides to suit the inclination of any individual. These books focus on routes toward a range of goals from health and spiritual well-being to personal success in your career. Publishers and bookshop owners say these books are among their best sellers. Self-help books have guided many away from contemporary confusion by pointing out the possible solutions available for the mystical seeker. The mystical seeker is *anyone* who looks beyond the dogmas and conventions that have bogged down both the potential of the individual and the progress of civilization. You may have pursued one or more of the following interests that can compose whole sections in bookstores:

Channeling	Visualization	Feng Shui
Epiphanies	Courses in Miracles	Everspring
Self-Actualization	Pendulums	Shamanism
Astrology	Numerology	Crystals

Tarot	Macrobiotics	Auras
Crystal Gazing	Gems and Stones	Angelolatry
Amulets	Talismans	Alternative Energies
Astral Projection	Biofeedback	Biorhythms
Reflexology	Inner Healing	Prana Ray Healing
Kinesiology	Reincarnation	Chanting
Witchcraft	Pyramidology	Shamanism
Out of Body Experiences		I Ching
Extra Sensory Perception		Various Meditation Disciplines

The foregoing is an incomplete list of the various paths toward well-being available to those of the do-it-yourself disposition. Undoubtedly, entirely new paths will develop with the new millennium. Although it cannot be determined at this time which alternative paths will endure, some doubtless will, just as some Chinese healing practices, once considered alternative, have established a permanent place in contemporary Western medicine. This book supports the use of many New Age consciousness pursuits that offer a way to fulfill one's potential. Many consciousness pilgrims investigate numerous programs just as many actors study varied techniques, assimilating and integrating them into their personal styles and making it difficult, sometimes, to tell which of their teachers have had the greatest influence on them.

The rise of new consciousness philosophies and disciplines is not the unprecedented phenomenon that it may seem. I am sure I share with many the belief that a good measure of it occurred when we passed through the events of the 20th century, aptly described as the most brutal, hideous and horrible century in history. In retaliation to the events of the recent millennium, many began to believe that traditional beliefs were no longer valid; some completely lost their religious beliefs. As a consequence, new consciousness beliefs began to burgeon as a way of both rebelling against established values and filling the spiritual vacuum left by the loss of religiosity. A creed has become clear: either we create a new century of higher consciousness and enlightenment, or we decay. (At the time of the printing of this book, the foreign terrorist attack on America should cause us to pause regarding the direction we will be taking into the 21st century.) In bookstores, self-help groups and elsewhere, people began to find answers and, for some, more than those they found in religious institutions. It should be added, though, that religious institutions have been also influenced by new consciousness beliefs and some are adding them to worship programs.

Much of what exists in present day higher consciousness beliefs is directly descended from Eastern religions and philosophies which the youthful in the 1960s embraced as a rebellion against the tragic and senseless Vietnam War. The change of consciousness was initially offered by Transcendental Mediation and was quickly seized by youth internationally who were happily swayed away from sensory pleasures. Eastern religions regard the senses as being a low level of consciousness and consequently teach that humanity's problem is that we are overly aware of our five senses and that these do not necessarily guide one to higher and more insightful planes of consciousness.

Unfortunately, the exploration of high levels of consciousness that began as retaliation for the low consciousness of the Vietnam War was regarded by certain segments in society as being spiritually dangerous and the exclusive domain of spaced-out freaks.

What is spirituality? Elizabeth Lesser, co-founder of the Omega Institute, says in her definitive *The New American Spirituality* that when she began her research she sent a questionnaire to hundreds of spiritual leaders, intellectuals and scientists, asking them their interpretation of the word spiritual. The answers she received led her to conclude that no one had *the* answer. Her conclusion was that what is spiritual for one person is not necessarily spiritual for another. Lesser believes that the spiritual search must be brave and fearless as it investigates reality. The intention of this book is to help you bravely and fearlessly search for a higher consciousness in your acting choices.

Much of an actor's search has to do with truth and reality and requires, as I have always proposed, going beyond oneself in order to reach one's fullest potential. Historically, artists have always been intrigued by spiritual elements, particularly those related to higher states of consciousness. Numerous creative people follow such paths in their natural stride in the attempt to discover a higher creative consciousness even if they are not necessarily in agreement as to what that higher consciousness might be. Sometimes, these people are a little ahead of their time and the course of civilization determines whether others will catch up sufficiently to share their vision. No one today, however, can fail to be aware of the advent of the enormous changes long predicted by visionaries. The best of today's new spirit is focusing on conserving the planet. This necessitates a shift of consciousness towards a spiritual level as we increasingly cherish the belief that we are on this earth as co-creators in a universal spirit, and, by fulfilling certain obligations, we improve upon our planet. George Gurdjieff, a pioneer in consciousness philosophy, believed that if we are unable to care for a plant or animal, we ultimately relinquish responsibility for each other and our planet's natural resources.

The new level of consciousness flowering on our struggling planet has taken many millennia to arrive. Stanislavski singled out the lack of spiritual content as the catalyst for humankind's destructiveness towards nature and emphasized that his System was based on observations of both human beings and nature. The decline of spiritual values in our civilization has reaped tragic consequences, including perhaps the daily occurrences of drive-by shootings, teen suicides, and school yard violence. Fortunately, there are contemporary philosophers among us who argue wisely that our instincts cause us to be repelled by cruelty and evil, to admire kindness, and to respect any person who has the courage to venture into new territories for the purpose of benefiting others and increasing mankind's skill and knowledge.

In acting, the spiritual and the mystical are interrelated. Some of the great actors of the past and present often have been described as being mystical or spiritual in their performances. For numerous artists, mysticism has been a personal confrontation of the conventional and the desire to illuminate the shadowed portions of their psyches. Van Gogh, for one, went into such "forbidden" territory in his time.

Strong currents of sensibility dictate that defying convention is perfectly acceptable for a painter, dancer, architect, composer or other artists. Unfortunately, protests arise when actors, practiced in long-accepted techniques, do likewise.

Venturing into the realm of the superconscious with the exercises herein is not a voodoo type of mysticism and neither is a performance of superconscious choices in a twilight zone of metaphysical mumbo-jumbo. There are performers, for example, with a superconscious spirit who seek a good performance by preceding it with a period of meditation or chanting in order to get into a superconscious state. That is not voodoo!

A narrow-minded belief exists that any kind of superconscious or mystical involvement in the acting process is delusional and deserves to be ridiculed. This belief is sometimes held by those who are addicted to external types of performance replete with vocal and physical clichés. Those who have been found guilty of haphazard technique and offensive conventionalities often have no notion how to contact creative wellsprings that will lead them toward a rebirth of technique—possibly more honest and truthful than one that has grown comfortably stale. No actor should be willing to go through an entire career without the realization of the heights of talent one has the potential to achieve. Reaching for the superconscious level in acting is not an easy matter. Just as an athlete must use physical muscles to shatter previous records, an actor must use superconscious "muscles" to break down barriers to the total creative awareness and growth in acting envisioned by Stanislavski as the "New Life."

There is a spiritual nature in all of us regardless of whether or not we choose to acknowledge it. It is part of our human nature.

TAPPING INTO YOUR SUPERCONSCIOUS

Blazing new trails in technique prowess will get you out of your own way, let in a new vitality and give you a feeling of creative purpose.

Any acting technique exercise you do, regardless of the particular discipline to which it may subscribe, calls for a state of creative consciousness. There are different levels of these states and you must decide whether to be prisoner to intractable beliefs about your technique principles or to be open to what may be a revelatory experience. It all depends on the strength of your desire to extend your creative quality and how far you are willing to go to experience other levels of awareness. All that you need to do is to awaken what already exists in you. Your impulses will do the rest and may even give you a "natural organic high" as you experience transformations. Your creative impulses contain all the resources you need to journey beyond and test the outer limits of conventional horizons.

With an "anything goes!" attitude, you will perceive what you need and also what you already have. As your capacity for self-evaluation expands, you will gain precise knowledge of the point to which your talent has already developed and the next level towards which it should progress. Your acting instrument will be strengthened by the recognition that your talent is becoming superior to anything you thought it could be; it will be further enlivened by looking forward to the even greater creative delights you will experience in the future.

The exercises herein offer you a way to discover energies for new experiences. They require you to reach deep within in order to create rushes of dramatic power. Permit that power to be fueled with passion as it surges out of you in such a way that there can be no doubt that you are being creative on a higher, more exhilarating, more imaginative level and that you are capable of creating both strong and delicate dynamics. By continually testing its limits, you stretch your instrument. Careful nurturing of your instrument goes hand and hand with the creative exploration of its deep meaning and, perhaps, its Stradavarian nature.

"If we do not push the limits and go where no man has gone before, then we stagnate," said an astronaut on the International Space Station. Stagnation is surely a feeling that you do not want to experience, ever. Stagnation brings total boredom; an inability to function; the loss of life's joy—all seems to be a void and only eventual death awaits. Tapping into your superconscious creative energies to open new vistas or artistry can certainly be an antidote.

This book contains guidelines for each exercise. Following are suggestions that apply to all exercises.

Bring to each exercise an interest in new and unusual acting technique experiences. Inevitably, as with sensory technique, locked-in emotions and impulses will makes themselves known. Permit them to be released. When letting yourself go to a strong experience, maintain control over it like a downhill skier flowing with the perils of a run while sustaining amazing control.

Selectivity and concentration are important ingredients. You should determine and control how much concentration is needed and the control of it. Overly intense concentration does not necessarily create the form of desired reality you seek.

There are numerous degrees of releasing a strong emotional experience. Sometimes it is a matter of reducing the intensity in order to arrive at desirable results. When Michelangelo was asked how he created his David, he said, "I just cut down until I found him." However, when you tone down a strong experience to discover how it can be used on a lower, confined level, it is desirable not to lose the essence of the experience at its strongest moment.

❂ ❂ ❂

METAMORPHOSIS

My body is my acting instrument.

EMBARKATION

Start from whatever state of being you are in even if you do not know what is happening in your new consciousness.

Try not to waiver when disembarking from your usual technique. Understanding will arrive as you journey deeper, and your constant quest will lead to a new consciousness reality. Trust it.

Approach each exercise in a state of awareness that permits your mind to wander with the richest use of your imagination. Stanislavski was convinced that an actor's imagination must be a powerful force to create imagery.

MAKING A BOLD STAND

Boldly propose a change to overcome any resistance you encounter. You can sense resistance if you feel that it is a struggle to explore another level of consciousness than you usually experience in your acting. Permit yourself to be shaken up.

Try not to have any preconceived notion of what you might discover. Your discovery might be more comfortable than the consciousness you are experiencing with your current technique.

Engage in rigorous self-examination. There is always a new prism for you to look through to change your perception.

Consider the new consciousness as an alternate way of inhabiting the consciousness of characters which you create.

EXPERIENCE

Let yourself be consumed by the experience of the exercises and relax into them as you explore, search and discover new creative insights about your new acting prowess.

Step into the new experiences that the exercises offer, leaving your old self behind.

When you sense a transformation while using your creative technique, permit your talent to go with it.

COMPLETION

Permit yourself to be a vessel for unusual experiences. If you experience something like riding on a speeding particle of light—so did Einstein at age 16. That kind of experience can offer you a flash of creative insight into your imagination.

Push your limits—go beyond the established boundaries of your talent and be obsessed with finding new challenges that offer deeper realities.

Believe that there are no limitations to your development of superconscious techniques.

Permit yourself to embrace an attitude of invincibility and the conviction that, with your imagination, you can accomplish the goal of each exercise.

Open yourself up to enjoying the journey. Compare the changes you experience with results from past choices. Are the new results dimensionally richer? Stronger? Are the results fresher than choices you have repeated many times in the past?

✿ ✿ ✿

AFFIRMATIONS

I will permit my body to become a creative tool. My body is my acting instrument. I can hone and harness it to function on a new artistic level of creative consciousness. I will liberate it from the past and move on.

The experience of an exercise already exists in me and is ready to be channeled towards artistic growth.

I know that reaching for higher forms of consciousness is not an easy matter and I am willing to work diligently and be disciplined to realize the boundless creative rewards that await me. I wish to offer to the exercises the exceptional in me.

I must be like an athlete who uses physical muscles to break down barriers in order to shatter a previous record. I must use my consciousness muscles to break down barriers so that I may reach total creative awareness.

INTO THE FUTURE

History, it might be said, continually moves forward and so do the techniques and skills needed for humankind's endeavors. The brimming promises of great discoveries in the new millennium are calling forth paradigm shifts in many fields. It is the obligation of actors to discover the ways of being a part of those shifts and a part of the future evolution of art techniques. The exercises in this book do not claim to be the be-all and end-all of acting technique possibilities, but they afford an avenue for actors to explore greater creative heights and move beyond the limits of what they expect or have been willing to accept. As you evolve in your quest, so does your potential for greater achievement.

My development and use of technique exercises have always been driven by my desire to innovate. I can only hope that the exercises engage you in a vision of being a part of the future through the realization that we are never finished in our development. Your duty to yourself is to capture the spirit of the times in which we live. That is accomplished by embracing what you personally think to be the best of established ways, but also breaking away from some of them as you create innovative paths for yourself. Our natural urge is to continually evolve and move forward. Not only can the exercises make your acting more interesting as you search for new technique functioning, they can also deepen your consciousness of the new millennium.

Constant nourishing of your consciousness will aid your ascent to higher unimaginable states. We are all works-in-progress with the urge to change the way things are done. Although, some believe it will take untold years before we can ascend to high states of consciousness, some strongly believe that they are now within our reach. As an evolved artist you are leading the exploration in mind and spirit expansion which may prove to be a silent weapon in global politics. World leaders are not sufficiently aware of the potential power of this weapon.

Do not be concerned with your flaws or that certain values in your present state of awareness are not as perfect as you wish. Even a higher force and stronger spirit than ours, whatever you may believe it to be, is not perfect if it, too, is constantly evolving and expanding. Nature itself seems to be on a quest for its own creative perfection, going beyond what exists and forever engaging in its own evolutionary progress with no end.

As an artist, and with the humility of a true artist, you have the obligation to bravely, fearlessly and aggressively move towards the path of higher states of creative consciousness. I hope that this book will help you to celebrate your acting creativity in a joyous new way as you dwell in the domain of Stanislavski's Fourth Level.

Part II

The Exercises

Part II:
The Exercises

TERMINOLOGY AND
ESSENTIAL ABBREVIATIONS

While developing the exercises in this book, I had to create an appropriate terminology, just as every emerging field creates its own language, computer terminology certainly being the foremost. In formulating the names, I did not ponder for any extended period of time. In retrospect, I recall that the names emerged spontaneously, often before the content of the exercises themselves.

For a complete list of exercise names, see the Table of Contents towards the front of this book.

Essential Abbreviations

Sp. Obj. - Spatial Objects

Ch. Imp. - Channeling Impulse
  OA: Original Area
  DA: Destination Area

IMO - Inner Moving Object

OSO - Outer Spatial Objects

P & P - Physiological and Psychological

PSO - Projected Spatial Object

DSO - Distant Spatial Object

Choices and Action Listings

The examples of choices and actions in this book were selected by actors with whom I have worked through the years. These actors were intrigued or felt compelled, or both, to go beyond sensory experiences in which they may have been previously trained or which I taught them. I have chosen examples used by my workshops actors for the unusual behavioral results achieved. However, you should attempt to formulate actions and choices that stem from your own personality and imagination and which you think are pertinent for a character you are interpreting.

Please remember that the examples in this book are those of other actors and are included to guide you in determining your own actions and choices. They are definitely not to be used as behavioral formulas of any kind, unless you feel, in some instances, an immediate connection to an example.

Improvising

Since this book can be used as a self-help acting workbook, it is suggested that when you work alone and experiment with the exercises, you should create or improvise a story, scenario or situation that is related to the action(s) and choice(s) you choose with each exercise. As such, you would improvise lines to say. You may, of course, select a character from a stage play or film script. It is not necessary that you memorize written dialogue. You can paraphrase the dialogue as you practice an exercise. (Anyway, memorization of any role should always follow the selection and practice of your action and choices.) With this procedure, you will not be doing the exercises in limbo, but will specifically relate them to a character in a dramatic situation. Additionally, it will be useful for you to verbally improvise dialogue to accompany the progress of an exercise. This will permit you to discover how your action and choices create a character's tonal quality. As in all the work based on the Stanislavski System, actions and choices must be seen in your acting instrument and heard in your voice.

SPATIAL OBJECTS EXERCISE

The central divisive issue concerning the use of the Stanislavski System has been the physical vs. the psychological. This initial exercise relates to the physical, that is, the outer manifestation of a character. The next chapter, the Channeling Impulse Exercise, relates to the character's inner life.

A fine stage or film actor senses the energies of the space surrounding a performance—the front, sides, above, beneath and behind. This sensing is easier to do in a theater performance than in motion pictures. In a theater performance, an actor becomes acquainted with a permanent performing environment. In motion pictures, the environment is always changing. Creating the realities of indoor and outdoor settings may require the actor's environment to change daily.

The Spatial Objects Exercise has helped actors summon and utilize spatial energies for as long as I have used it in my teachings. In today's context, the exercise also offers an imaginative tool film actors can use when performing in the "unreal" empty spaces of digital films.

The use of digital technology in motion pictures is gaining momentum, just as it is changing other forms of art including painting and sculpture. The advance of digital films reflects the increasingly sophisticated uses of technology in today's quickly changing world, and, as a palette of technologies, will transform the way many motion pictures will be created. With the establishment of digital film departments in universities, the filmmakers of tomorrow are being groomed to make full use of the potentials of digital technologies. Student films, which traditionally have used both beginning and experienced actors in a realistic manner and in realistic settings, may give many actors their first experience with digital films.

Digital filmmaking presents a new set of demands for film actors. Digital technologies require the actor to have a different conception of spatial entities while performing. Actors who have worked in high-tech films have related their encounters with the accoutrements of digital films and how they imaginatively met the challenge of entering into bare settings and merging with the voids and abysses of digital sets, often contributing brilliant touches to a situation. The creative exploration of the potential of digital filmmaking is only possible when the actor goes beyond traditional limitations, a goal which permeates the philosophy and intent of this book.

Will there soon be a demand for digital camera acting classes? It is not beyond the realm of possibilities given the already enormous range of workshops in Hollywood. Only the future will reveal the total impact of digital technologies, but the overall consensus about this situation is that the trained actor will not only need to be able to cope with what is real—just as actors have done since the birth of theater arts—but also to function creatively with the virtual characters, settings, and images of digital films. This expectation will, without doubt, become omnipresent as time progresses.

The dawn of the digital age has coincided with an increased emphasis on the physical aspect in acting. The Spatial Objects Exercise has as its major purpose to help both the stage and film actor physicalize to a greater degree. The Spatial Objects Exercise is very much in harmony with the presence of the technological equipment used in digital films, offering the creative impulse necessary for the film actor to deal spatially with the wires, gadgets and other encompassing paraphernalia required for digital filming.

Exercises of sensorial stimulation in the Stanislavski System relates to how we are affected by various stimuli in the environment: odors, sounds, sights, objects, and varying degrees of temperature. The Spatial Objects Exercise creates environmental forces which are registered as tactile experiences, but are not necessarily registered in sensorial experiences—such as cold, heat, warm breeze, rain, etc. However, your imagination can create them and make them exist as strongly as any sensory experience. When you refer to the suggestions for choices for the exercise, it will be evident that the exercise is intended to endow tactile energies to the imaginary objects that contact you.

Your creative consciousness is capable of experiencing new and imaginary realities. Your actual sensory realities are limited to your real-life experiences and enable you to create the physical life of a character. The Spatial Objects Exercise deals with imaginary realities that you create and which permit you to experience sensations which you were not consciously aware you could have. This exercise also greatly multiplies the tactile stimuli available for physical behavior and sensations. For that reason, latent visceral qualities will open up with new physical nuances and more imaginative texture. In other words, this exercise will create the multi-nuanced physicalities of a character and give it a greater dimension.

Your willingness to experience your choices will aid in creating behavior that is fresh, spontaneous and unpredictable.

The nature of your choices for this exercise should be tactile; there is no need to dwell on other sensorial aspects of the objects. The aim of the exercise is to enable you to extend your range of tactile experiences. This requires creating imaginary phenomena that can have powerful realities. A new mode of consciousness develops as you become more acquainted with the existence of new streams of energy enveloping you.

As an experimental choice for a character you are creating, the use of this exercise can be illuminating. Part of role building is to know how the character relates to space and its boundaries. This exercise is not unlike working with the expanding or narrowing Circles of Attention that Stanislavski describes in *An Actor Prepares*.

In sensorial techniques used to create tactile physicalities, an actor selects choices from familiar environmental experiences. In the Spatial Objects Exercise, you can use a fantasy approach and create a variety of imaginary forces. The imaginary forces you contact can shape your acting instrument and produce an unusual behavioral presence.

Renowned physicists have viewed the macroscopic space that surrounds us and have explained how space vibrates with activities which are part of our existence. Some physicists have been particularly drawn to the Zen concept of space being a breathing and living continuum. For example, the aesthetics of Zen painting calls on one to enter into a painting and sense its motion.

In this exercise you acquaint yourself with the dynamic and unseen forces that perpetually besiege the human condition. Our multitude of nerve endings are constantly having tactile contact with these unseen energy streams. They are powerful because, to a great extent, we depend upon them to trigger our energy sources. Some elements in our environment are composed of cosmic energies which give us sustenance. We draw them into our body for the same reason that we drink water or eat food. The Spatial Objects Exercise will demonstrate how aspects of your human conditioning make you aware or unaware of invisible forces acting upon you.

The choices for the exercise should affect the entire body. Your primary concern is to acquire knowledge for creating a new language in the acting space you inhabit. The exercise also has a way of specifically pointing out your vulnerabilities and defenses. As a result, you might form boundaries or barriers preventing the energies of your Spatial Objects from making tactile contact with your body. You resolve that by dissolving those limiting factors, thereby leaving yourself open to the tactile experience possible through the Spatial Objects Exercise.

THE SPATIAL OBJECTS EXERCISE

1. Select an action which conveys the motivation and meaning you wish to examine.

2. Select a Spatial Objects choice from the following suggestions or create your own after reviewing the list.

ACTION	SPATIAL OBJECTS
To admire	Different color balloons
To remain on my feet	Flying arrows
To figure out	Abstract paintings
To reject	Infectious people
To hesitate	Spears
To smash	Spider webs
To find protection	Blankets
To cast off the yoke	Bugs
To see beyond	Mirrors
To put something over	Masks
To take a chance	Nazi SS officers with machine guns
To scorn	Syringes
To fight poachers	Wounded animals
To win them over	Scooping seagulls
To cool things off	Sticks of burning incense

ACTION	SPATIAL OBJECTS
To resist	Darts
To brush off	Corn silk
To be self-concerned	Barbed wire
To make light of inner pain	Pounding fists
To keep things my way	Falcons
To win my place	Jabbing fingers
To obscure	Hypnotizing hands
To squirm through	Unknown faces
To persevere	Gremlins with sticking pins
To discover the truth	Waves of knowledge
To surmount	Rocks of different sizes
To have the power	Particles of comet tails
To deliver a message	Giant slimy squids
To stay in my own world	Large cotton balls

MORE CHOICE SELECTIONS

Friendly spirits	Meteors
Knives	Needles
Various hands	Lasso ropes
Tumbleweed	Religious spirits
Pellets of steam	Birds
Slimy walls	Pieces of flesh
Giant hammers	Swirls of chiffon
Snowballs	Colony of lepers
Electrical sparks	Bees

Licking tongues

Sticky rubber objects

Laughing mouths

Spotlights

Slow-moving bubbles

Floating balloons

Giant dollar bills

Sexual organs

A person duplicated

Little green men

Caressing hands

Hands of children

Man-eating ants

Snakes

Feather dusters

Light beams

Mouths

Cotton puffs

Down pillows

Aurora Borealis

Swarm of honey bees

Festered demons

Jet fighter planes

Green hay

Sound waves of yelling

Cat crap

Cold earth worms

Ice cubes

Fighter planes

Plants

Fantasy objects

Animal eyes

Holographs

Frisbees

Clouds

Cosmic rays

Feathers

Globs of Jello

Butterfly wings

Red and green flashing lights

Stubby fingers

Hovering knives

Silver cords

Sacred tablets

Wood carvings

People applauding and booing

Spiderwebs

Tarantulas

Tickling fingers

Different colored balloons

Sound waves of violins

Miniature Angels

GUIDELINES FOR THE
SPATIAL OBJECTS EXERCISE

...You do not make direct contact with your choice with your hands or other parts of your body. You grant your choice the freedom to make contact with you. A helpful image from nature is the way wind sculpts sand dunes with varying shapes and forms. Let your choices have the varying rhythmic powers of wind as you permit the objects to be a shaping force and give your instrument fluid forms. Imagine the objects as tools belonging to a sculptor and your body as the material upon which the tools create living shapes. As you may have concluded, this exercise attempts to depart from the usual results often attained by overall sensorial sensations of heat, cold, etc.

...Permit Spatial Objects to engulf you as they approach you from above, below, back, front and sides; permit them to contact you at different angles. Let the space around you breathe with the energies of your choices as they contact you with varying degrees of force or tenderness. Let the choices agitate your acting instrument; experience the texture of the physical impulses they create. The important factor is to get involved with the objects as they affect every part of your body. By submitting your body completely to the objects, you will gain a new ability to create within your imagination tactile behavior unlike any you may have previously experienced.

...Permit yourself to be surrounded by objects that are trying to envelop you in ways that can be loving, destructive or mystifying. Let the objects break through any barriers you have consciously or unconsciously created between your body and the objects. Even if you do not particularly enjoy the nature of certain objects, go with your imagination and discover how the spatial abrasion inherent in objectionable objects can give you a stronger presence.

...Avoid contacting the objects visually. Let the objects contact you without attempting to see them. Be like a child with your choices. A child creates toys out of a variety of objects by permitting them to be playful.

...Permit the objects to have different rhythms and motions. Can they assail you so strongly that standing becomes difficult? Can they make you melt away? Do you have faith in the power of the objects that contact and surround you? You have created them within your fantasy and now must believe in their presence and realities.

...After you have completed a few exercises, you no longer need to submit your body completely to the objects. There can now be mutual exploration between the objects and your muscles, limbs, etc. Develop a sense of your body parts having a lively interaction with the objects. If certain choices cause parts of your body to contract, you can rid yourself of any tightness by using the muscles of the contracted area (such as the stomach, torso or pelvis) to contact the object.

...Negative choices can affect you, but don't shrink away or physically tense up. If you do, the behavioral results you seek will be diminished. For a richly complex and sensitive action, permit choices in the space around you to affect you in varying ways: loving, hateful, aggressive, sexual, fearful, etc.

...You can also duplicate a single object many times in your imagination. You may wish, for example, to duplicate a person so that there are numerous "clones" of the person. If you are duplicating parts of a person, let the parts relate to visible or hidden feelings you have about the person. You can also permit parts of a person (e.g. hands, lips, erotic parts) to proclaim feelings the person has about you. Any mixed feelings about a certain part of a person (maybe you don't like the person's nose) will lead you to multi-layered nuances. Let various parts of a person contact you in different ways—lovingly on your face, suspiciously on your back and aggressively in your pelvic area.

...The exercise can reveal fixed behavior—the involvement or lack of involvement you have in your daily life. Discover any possible fixed role you may have in your spatial orientation and how environmental objects affect you with feelings of isolation, intense sexuality, claustrophobia, etc. Determine which objects you will not permit to enter into your spatial world and the reasons for their exclusion. Then permit the objects to enter into your space, make contact with you and affect you in a way which you perhaps have never experienced.

...You can also work with sensory characteristics of the objects. Once you have established the tactile response, focus on other ways of being stimulated by your choice. Create the sound of the objects as they approach you. Imagine how they smell. Establish their taste as they enter or try to enter your mouth. Experience sound differently as the objects plug up your ears.

Some actors don't know one part of their body from another. The bottom line of the exercise is, therefore, an enhanced richness of expression in every part of your body. Don't be an actor who doesn't know one's butt from one's elbow. "Acting is to perform, to be the part; to be it in your arms, your legs; to be what you are acting; to be it all over, that is acting," said the Irish-American dramatist and actor Dion Boucicault.

CHANNELING IMPULSE EXERCISE

Strasberg at the Actors Studio (edited by Robert Hethmon), Harold Clurman's *The Fervent Years* and Elia Kazan's *A Life* are required reading for a solid knowledge of the American adaptation of the Stanislavski System.

In the index to *Strasberg at the Actors Studio,* there are more entries under "Impulses" than under any other subject. Strasberg's focus on impulses was a paramount catalyst for my ongoing journey as teacher and researcher. I have always known that impulses, as ingrained functions of an acting talent, are strengthened with sensory exercises. Yet, in my study with notable teachers of the Stanislavski System and in extensive research in the field, I discovered that no technique exercise had been developed specifically to strengthen acting impulses beyond their natural sensorial presence in an actor. Very early in my work with actors, I began to formulate a relevant impulse exercise to accomplish that goal. My desire to see exercises created and utilized to enhance and fine tune the use of impulses propelled my initial forays into the development of a group of exercises focused on achieving greater sensorial consciousness. My efforts were instantly rewarded when talented and seasoned actors created clear and unequivocal values during their first experience with the Channeling Impulse Exercise.

The Channeling Impulse Exercise will permit you to sense the flow of new inner energy patterns, transforming the use of your inner sensitivities. This transformation can give you increased creative control of your flow of inner energies and help you create a new artistic image. Doing so requires that you be open to the risks involved in changing your creative style, without fearing the step into the unknown.

Picasso was not afraid when he gave up cubism to advance through a succession of creative changes, even though he was putting his reputation as an established artist at risk. Like other modern artists, he began with still lifes of simple, everyday subjects—pitcher and apples, bowl and fruit—transformed with the cubist vision of their form, color, and composition.

The Stanislavski sensory exercises of taste, smell and pain contact personal experiences you have had with the inner senses in order to give authenticity to your emotional behavior. The meanings you derived from those exercises are important to the Channeling Impulse Exercise. Often a localized sensorial sensation is the beginning point for this exercise. From there, its energy is transmitted to other inner areas. While the sensory exercises created behavior that related to your own inner impulses, the Channeling Impulse Exercise creates unfamiliar impulses that are, nevertheless, part of your organic instrument. This exercise will compel you to question your familiar impulses and discover deeper, hidden areas which will give your impulses fresher meanings.

With this exercise, you will begin to strengthen your response to an increasing range of unfamiliar experiences. You have dwelled in your body for some time and may be familiar with its sensory experiences, but suddenly you will discover that your inner organs, connecting tissues, autonomic nervous system and myriad cells can be charged with new energies.

Ordinarily, we feel only aches and pains that have to do with certain disturbances that take place within the body. Aside from the pleasures of the stomach, we take too much for granted how the organs are feeling the rest of the time. With the Channeling Impulse Exercise you will be able to give the inner organs new experiences. The sensations you will feel in your organs will create transformative energies as they proceed to circulate through the countless channels of your organic physical and chemical systems. The organs are part of your inner self and can be imaginatively explored for new and unfamiliar choices. You might even achieve a new understanding of the function of your inner organs and the purpose of their existence in terms of your inner life.

This exercise finds meaning in the following increasingly accepted forms of personal growth experiences and alternative medicine techniques:

Acupuncture

Acupuncture and acupressure use the body's own energy to produce a healing flow through the myriad channels in the body. Although Western science has not been able to totally explain how acupuncture works, it has become more accepting of this valuable medical treatment.

Yoga

The Channeling Impulse Exercise is related to the yogic principle of transferring energies. In yoga, the pituitary gland (located at the base of the brain) can be stimulated to secrete beneficial hormones into the entire body. Stanislavski studied yoga and attempted to use its principles in the development of his System. Many never shared his interest in yoga, although his widely-used Circles of Attention exercise was inspired by yogic principles.

Biofeedback

This innovative discipline can improve poor circulation simply by creating warmth in one area of the body and permitting the warmth to be channeled to cold areas afflicted with poor circulation.

Psychic Energy

The energy of top young actors has both physical and psychic qualities. Perhaps, the glow of their physical persona has something to do with their psychic energy. Practitioners of psychic energy create strong, healthy auras surrounding an inner organ, such as the heart, and then permit its healthy glow to be channeled into the rest of the body.

Perhaps you have begun to regard this exercise as a tool which is not only creative but also holistically beneficial for the tip-top state of health that an actor must possess. This exercise offers a double blessing, since through its use you can create an acting choice and simultaneously improve your well-being. The electricity of an actor's impulses plays a vital part in communicating with an audience or camera. In addition, psychological and physical attitudes can change in richness and intensity as the impulse is channeled from one area to another. These electrical impulses are present in the body's multitudinous cells. As an actor, you should want to know how to become acquainted with the nature of these impulses.

Therapeutic insights and benefits can be derived from the exercise. By pointing out how you may be blocking certain impulses, the exercise grants you the means to unblock them and complete their expressive nature. You also have the opportunity to examine the nature and consequences of blocked impulses. You can even discover how certain blocked emotions, such as aggression, can be good for your well-being as you unleash it and let it travel through your body. Strongly blocked emotions definitely restrict the creative use of your instrument. In my workshop, I have encountered actors conditioned to avoid the expression of aggressive emotions. The goal for such people is not to regard the emotion in a negative way but to find out about its positive aspects.

Be prepared for a sudden change in the quality of your acting experience. Even actors who have not fully responded to sensory exercises find with the Channeling Impulse Exercise that floodgates suddenly open as the richness of their sensitivities begins to be used in a more imaginative and creative way. This exercise, therefore, offers invaluable means to deal with problems of feelings that were not refined during the sensory work.

Finally, the best acting occurs when a true relationship between impulse and expression replaces uncontrolled emotion. This exercise intends to give you the artistic skill to create that desirable relationship.

THE CHANNELING IMPULSE EXERCISE

You may wish to refer to the examples which begin on page 64 in order to have a fuller image of the essence of a Channeling Impulse.

1. Select an action. (An action list appears in the Appendix.)

2. Select an emotion for the action.

Love	Envy
Tenderness	Impatience
Sexual Excitement	Obstinacy
Sympathy	Guilt
Pity	Despair
Anxiety	Anger
Shame	Helplessness
Sadness	Joy

Confidence	Hope
Pride	Passion
Hopelessness	Hate
Greed	Serenity
Fear	Depression
Rage	Numbness
Courage	Compassion
Flippancy	Peevishness
Laughter	Conviction

3. Select a sensation, sensory or otherwise, which you feel is related to the emotion.

4. Select an original area and a destination area, as explained in the guidelines on page 65.

EXAMPLES

To get all I can
Emotion: Anxiety
Original area: Itchy feet
Destination area: Face

To plow through the blizzard
Emotion: Impatience
Original area: Power line buzz in right hand
Destination area: Left calf

To provoke
Emotion: Tenderness
Original area: Taste in mouth
Destination area: Chest

To listen
Emotion: Sadness
Original area: Sensation in left knee
Destination area: Chin

To hold my ground
Emotion: Pride
Original area: Hot oil in crotch
Destination area: Cheek bones

To cool things off
Emotion: Sadness
Original area: Howling winds in thighs
Destination area: Inside of eyeballs

To blow it all up
Emotion: Rage
Original area: Fire in eyes
Destination area: Stomach

To free their minds
Emotion: Serenity
Original area: Third eye
Destination area: Left palm

Guidelines for the Channeling Impulse Exercise

...Permit the choice to reside in a localized area somewhere in the body. This is referred to as the *original area* where you internally experience the nature of the choice. Don't be afraid of using unfamiliar sensations in the original area. You can even select and reproduce an experience which has occurred in another part of

your body as some of the examples will illustrate.
...It is preferable and more effective to create
sensations originating inside the body. Therefore,
if you choose an external choice, such as sun on
the head, it is important that the sensation move
inside the head.
...Maintain the sensation in the original area
while relaxing the rest of the body, particularly
the *destination area* to which you will first
channel the impulse. Be mindful of any antici-
pated sensation in the destination area. The ability to maintain the sensation is not dissimilar to
that of the giant iguanas of the Galapagos Islands
who can bring their blood to their center to con-
serve body heat.
...Do not rush the exercise by releasing it without sufficient exploration in either the original
area or the destination area.
...Release the sensation from the original area
and allow it to travel through areas of relaxation
into the destination area. If the sensation has
been strong in the original area, it should be
strong when arriving at the destination area. If
not, you may be retaining some of the sensation
in the original area.
...When you have channeled the sensation into
the destination area, relax the original area and
other areas through which the sensation has traveled on its way to the destination area. The sensation now replicates itself in the destination
area. Sense the change that is caused in the destination area. Permit it to remain there as long
as you wish.
...Release the sensation from the destination

area and let it travel in the body, journeying to wherever it wishes. For a specific behavioral purpose, you can release the sensation from the destination area on a particular word or line of dialogue. As described by those who had seen her perform, the immortal Italian actress Eleanora Duse was noted as having the ability to begin a sensation in her toes and then move it upwards into her head area before releasing it into her famous smile.

...For subtle behavioral purposes, create the sensation in an area and release small amounts of it into another area. For example, gradually let a sensation in the stomach rise to the face. A certain expression on the face can be gradually increased in strength as more sensation from the stomach rises to the face area. This can be particularly useful for a film close-up given the ability of a camera to capture subtle changes in facial changes such as heat rising from the torso to the cheeks and remaining there as long as desired.

...When the sensation has been released from the destination area, play with it over long distances as it travels from one area of the body to another. Determine the way in which your selected emotion is affected as the impulse moves around. Is it intensified or weakened? If it weakens, it may become intensified again upon moving the impulse into another area. These different experiences create nuanced behavior.

...Re-examine the destination area. Has all of the sensation been released?

...As the energy of the impulse courses its way through your system, be intrigued by the physical and psychological effects. Sense the electrical communication of the nerve cells in the nervous system as an impulse shoots from one area to another. Trap it in areas and later release it to another area of entrapment.

...Let the impulse energize the extremities. The impulse can affect the fingers and create spontaneous gestural detail.

...Create the rhythms desired as you transmit the sensation of your choice. Be aware of your ability to steer the impulses so that they do not go out of control. Sometimes a talent can become confused by the rich response to certain impulses. This exercise offers a way of dealing with that concern.

...When you experience a sensation or stimulus in life, such as a lump in the throat or butterflies in the stomach, immediately channel that sensation elsewhere. You may discover that the sensation can have the same intensity in other inner areas or that the sensation might even be stronger in another area.

...In later stages of experimenting with this exercise, omit the destination area and permit the sensation of the original area to suddenly spread out through the entire body at once.

There are numerous ways to experiment with the Channeling Impulse Exercise. As you express your own individuality, you will, naturally, arrive at your own ideas.

EXAMPLES

Emotion	Choice in Original Area	Destination Area
Love	Warmth in pelvis	Eyes
Laughter	Itch on top of head	Throat
Compassion	Brilliant warmth in stomach	Head
Fear	Sharpness in solar plexus	Shoulders
Flippancy	Flame in genitals	Top of head
Envy	Cold hand	Eyes
Pride	Taste in mouth	Back of neck
Anxiety	Severe pain in groin	Head
Hopelessness	Taste in mouth	Stomach
Impatience	Itch in left toe	Both hands
Sympathy	Objects in hand	Back of neck
Tenderness	Taste in mouth	Chest
Greed	Itchy hand	Both feet
Depression	Upset stomach	Head
Courage	Electric current in arms	Entire body
Sexuality	Anatomical object in pelvis	Hands
Rage	Fire in chest	Head
Despair	Bitter taste in mouth	Stomach
Joy	Sound in solar plexus	Cheeks
Pride	Hot tension in tailbone	Eyes
Guilt	Flutter in heart	Thighs
Confidence	Warm beam of light in base of brain	Base of spine

Emotion	Choice in Original Area	Destination Area
Serenity	Sunshine inside head	Extremities
Peevishness	Cold chill in spine	Eyes
Pity	Electricity in sinuses	Feet
Numbness	Icy cheeks	Abdomen

CHOICES FOR ORIGINAL AND DESTINATION AREAS

HEAD

Headache to stomach

Itch on top of head to throat

Warmth in head to heart

Explosion in head to hands

Headache to mouth

Sound in head to pelvis

Sound in head to stomach

Pounding in brain to stomach

Warm oil in head to hands

Brilliant light in head to hands

Sun in head to body

OTHER HEAD AREAS

Aching in jaw to temples

Numbness in lips to chest

Tension in temples to stomach

Pain in eyes to back

Taste in mouth to back of neck

Tightness between temples to legs

Burning in eyes to stomach

Pain in jaw to forehead

Stiffness in jaw to stomach

Sunshine in head to legs

Pain in cheekbones to eyes

Throbbing in temples to legs

Sound in heart to Third eye

White light in ears to knees

Perfume in sinus to throat and chest

Debussy music in ears to hands and fingers

NECK AND THROAT

Warmth in back of neck to throat

Warmth in neck to shoulder

Neckache to small of back

Dry throat to stomach

Taste in throat to lips

Pain in neck to face

Energy in neck to eyes

Tightness in throat to feet

Thirst in throat to ears

Tears in throat to eyes

SHOULDER

Warmth in shoulder blade to forehead

Cold in left shoulder to hands

Energy in shoulder to arms and hands

Pain in right shoulder to head

Stiffness in shoulder to face

Sensation in one shoulder to other shoulder

CHEST

Warm chest to back of neck

Sexual feeling in chest area to eyes

Numbness in breast to face

Tightness in chest to cheekbones

Heat in chest to face and ears

Low energy charge in chest to legs

Fire from chest to head

HEART

Energy from heart to Third eye

Erratic heartbeat to legs

Palpitations to head

Strong, steady heartbeat to head

Heartache to mouth and hands

Racing heart to head

Heartache to hands

Rapid heartbeat to upper spine

Flutter in heart to thighs

ABDOMINAL AREA

Nausea in stomach to feet

Upset stomach to face

Laughter from diaphragm to face

Full stomach to base of brain

Butterflies in stomach to face

Hunger pangs in stomach to pelvic area

Nervous stomach to eyes

Electricity from stomach to eyes

Stomachache to eyeballs

Electric energy from stomach to throat

Queasiness in stomach to fingertips

Full stomach to armpits

Brilliant warmth in stomach to head

Queasiness in stomach to temples

Fullness in stomach to face

Stomachache to head

Cramps in stomach to legs

Sensation in lower intestine to chest cavity

Burning sensation in stomach to eyes

Cold water in navel to toe tips

BACK AND SIDES

Cold chill up spine and through eyes

Stiffness in spine to neck

Pain in back to face

Energy from lower spine to face

Ache in left side to both shoulders

Warmth from base of spine up through spinal column and into head

Ice water up and down spine

PELVIS AND GROIN

Sensation in pelvis to left hand

Sensation in pelvis to eyes

Pain in groin to head

Sensation in groin to eyes

Hot wine in the veins to heart

Soreness in pelvis to eyes

GENITALIA

Sexual arousal in male organ to chest and shoulders

Sexual excitement in clitoris to throat

Warm genitals to face

Arousal in genitals into the veins

Horny hot flashes in genitals to eyes

Sensation in crotch to top of head

ARMS AND HANDS

Nervous fingers to bridge of nose

Pain in hand to face

Itchy hand to nose

Warmth in hand to shoulders

Clammy hand to back of neck

Sensation in upper arm to eyes

Heat in thumb to chest

Numbness in hand to feet

Electric current in arm into body

LEGS AND FEET

Sensation in legs to cheekbones

Tickling foot to nose

Itchy foot to the leg

Stiffness in knee to shoulders

Warmth in foot to head

Itchy foot to mouth

Itchy foot to hands

Pain in foot to stomach

Cold foot to chest

Numbness in foot to arms

Tingling in foot to throat

Warmth in thigh to face

INTROJECTION EXERCISE

The process of introjecting people into the fabric of our personalities can formulate indelible traits. It is a process we all undergo. The actor also has this experience whenever attempting to enter into the inner and outer essence of a character. The creative power of introjecting another person permits you to fully charge yourself by creating behavior very different from that which would arise from your own personality. Being able to completely step out of oneself and into the skin of a character is an actor's ultimate artistic satisfaction and, for many, the very reason why they have become actors.

Certain actors have a very special gift for mimicking others—an uncanny ability to capture both the physical and vocal qualities of another person. Robert Duvall credits his mother's superb ability to mimic others as foundational to his own engrossing sense of character. In mimicry, some actors can accurately adopt the physical looks; others can precisely imitate the vocal. However, not all have the ability to combine the physical with the vocal which this exercise aspires to develop.

The process of introjecting people for creative and other purposes is an ancient one. Alexander the Great introjected the image he had of the legendary warrior Achilles; Leonardo da Vinci followed people around for hours and introjected physical expressions which he incorporated into his painting of *The Last Supper.*

Napoleon was trained by a professional actor to "act" like an emperor. Therapeutic and spiritual growth programs encourage one to summon the spirit of another who has qualities that are desired. This could be a religious figure or even Rembrandt, Einstein or a remarkable athlete. A devout Christian sees Christ in every person, even in a street person—perhaps especially so. By such spiritual practice, a Christian enters into a Christ consciousness in the same way that a Buddhist enters into a Buddha consciousness. The eminent musician Ray Charles introjected Nat King Cole. Charles said that he breathed Cole, ate him, drank him and tasted him day and night until he was able to find his own style of musicianship.

Well-known actors regard introjecting as a "stealing process." Some even admit they have stolen from admired performances given by other actors. Chameleon actors often use other actors to change their looks and personality. Stravinsky admitted "stealing" from Mozart but claimed that he had the right to do so because he loved Mozart's music. When film critic David Denby speculated that Peter O'Toole incorporated traits of Richard Burton, John Barrymore and Errol Flynn for his stylish performance in *My Favorite Year,* he was acknowledging O'Toole's undoubted right to do so. Perhaps the final word rests with Francisco de Goya who advised his daughter to paint reproductions of the old masters and said, "Copying is good; it loosens the hand." For a painter, a "loose" hand is of supreme importance. In the same context, introjecting other people loosens the actor's body.

The use of introjection in the career of outstanding performers is enlightening:

Marlon Brando once said, "Actors have to observe, and I enjoy that part of it. They have to know how much spit you've got in your mouth and where the weight of your elbows is. I could sit all day in the Optimo Cigar Store telephone booth on 42nd Street and just watch the people pass by."

As with any actor who infixes the behavioral characteristics of other people, Brando's observations are stored away for present and future use.

Alec Guiness related, "When I was a young student...I took to following people because some instinct in me said, 'Follow! You may find out something about that person.' That is what I used to do one hour each day, like a detective...I'd begin to be in the kind of mood they were in, and beyond mood, know something of their nature."

Laurence Olivier introjected Americans to great advantage. At the beginning of his career his role model was the Milwaukee-born actor Alfred Lunt. During the creation of the title role in *Richard III,* Olivier introjected the American director Jed Harris, whom he referred to as the most repulsive person he had ever worked with.

Robert DeNiro, in the early stages of his career, carefully studied all of Brando's films. Jeremy Irons said that he has emulated different actors to achieve certain qualities in his personal style and mentions Olivier, Guiness, Brando,

O'Toole and Paul Scofield.

The magnificent diva Maria Callas resorted to an introjection process after a cruel critic in Verona reviewed her performance in *Aida*. He wrote that he couldn't distinguish her legs from the legs of the elephants on stage. She vowed to shed her obesity and took the slim Audrey Hepburn as an introjection image. Callas' eventual physical transformation stunned everyone.

Helen Hayes used her own grandmother as a pattern for her most well-known stage role of Queen Victoria. On a London street, her grandmother had seen Queen Victoria's wedding procession passing by, and, over a period of time had adopted some of the Queen's traits.

After 20 years in regional and summer theatres, the incomparable Sada Thompson, achieved overnight Broadway stardom in the play *Twigs,* in which she portrayed four different characters with startling dissimilarities. She said that during rehearsals she had to get inside the characters and often thought of people she knew, like her grandmother and neighbors. She thought of them constantly so that they gradually seeped into her and took over.

Guidelines for the Introjection Exercise

...When you introject someone important in your life, determine how you are affected by that person's particular psyche. Is it beneficial or deleterious? Make an effort to get the interior sense of the person. Create the particular sensory realities that the person has. By recreating the inner life you also will make direct contact with the drives of that individual's personality.

...You can also introject a singular feature of a person, e.g., the way a person smiles, gestures or walks.

...During our work together, Cicely Tyson told me that, in order to feel a character, she had to get under the character's skin until it was skintight. This points out the creative desirability of feeling as you own the skin and nerves of an introject. With this kind of exploration, the introject of the person will posses you and shape behavioral elements.

...Actors are typically observant—and often extremely compassionate—in their relations with people from every walk of life. Every person gains significance as a possible model of human behavior. Each day, the TV news shows displays salt-of-the-earth people conveying great emotional power in response to events in their lives. Get inside the human simplicity of an unsophisticated and plain person who arouses your interest and compassion. Attempt to make direct contact with that person's inner experience and feelings. Soak up the individual's gestural language. By doing so, you form a psychobiography about the person's inner self.

...Use your actor's keen powers of observation to create behavioral details that have to do with the stimuli and phobias that affect an introject: rapid heart beat, perspiring hands, butterflies in the stomach, weakness in the knees. (Other stimuli choices are listed in *All About Method Acting*.) Try to create the rush of adrenalin that goes through a person when a panic attack is triggered. When defining a stimulus such as butterflies in the stomach, create butterflies with a long wing span to sense the distress of such a stimulus. In dealing with an introject's phobias, try to understand how phobias can create extreme feelings of hyperventilation, bringing you almost to the edge of fainting.

THE INTROCOMBO EXERCISE

For this exercise you combine traits of several people to approximate your image of a particular character for whom a single introject will not give you all the tangibles. The personalities you introject can be from different periods in time, or a mixture of past, present and, with enough imagination, even the future! The material to accomplish an unusual IntroCombo Exercise may exist entirely in your imagination or may benefit from conscientious research.

EXAMPLES

(Numbered examples offer the areas specific to each of your introjects.)

To discover a new way
1. Head and voice
2. Arms and hands
3. Hips

To search for what I want
1. Facial
2. Arms, hands and legs
3. Torso

To calm their anxieties
1. Eyes and mouth
2. Hands and shoulders
3. Legs

To explain it all the way
1. Brain and mouth
2. Eyes and head movements
3. Hands and arms
4. Legs

In the creation of a character, sometimes you may only wish to use external features of a person and at other times, only the interior—or you can create a mixture of external and internal features. The introjection of a person's facial features can automatically summon forth other features of the person.

THE INTROCOMBO-COMBO EXERCISE

In this exercise, you depart from what may seem like simple patterning and compose bold and complex characters. You add other exercises to your introjects which alone may not give you the complete sense of a character. Added exercises can enhance a character's unusual feature.

EXAMPLES

To tantalize
1. Head and hands
2. Rest of body
Ch. Imp. - Confidence
    OA - Pacific Ocean air in head
    DA - Knees

To nurture
1. Mouth and eyes
2. Arms and legs
Sp. Obj.- Sound waves of music

To question
1. Head, neck and shoulders
2. Entire body below the neck
Sp. Obj. - Eyes and numbers

In my workshop, I have observed that the Introjection Exercise can be more useful than the Characterization Exercise described in *All About Method Acting.*

The Characterization Exercise is extremely useful when you are not able to introject features of certain people for a character you are creating.

INNER MOVING OBJECT EXERCISE

The Inner Moving Object Exercise strengthens and deepens your internal dynamics and will enrich your inner values with a fresh potency. There are numerous moments in the creation of a character when the interior life dominates dramatically. An audience and a camera can sense its palpability. Any role you interpret will inevitably have moments that convey only the inner life of the character.

When you wish to expose the deepest of feelings, you may discover the Inner Moving Object Exercise to be a golden key. When an object surges within you and ignites an inner space, you will become aware of its help in tapping into the internal disturbance or hidden elation of a character.

Fine actors have a very special gift for creating the complex interior of a character without utilizing outward behavior and gestures. The quality of the interior life thusly portrayed conveys that something more is present than that which is outwardly seen and heard.

Lillian Gish, whose award winning film career covered a span of nearly 80 years, was an actress of supreme talent and, assuredly, phenomenal career longevity! You should acquaint yourself with her transcendent film performances, from *Broken Blossoms* (1915) to *All the Way Home* (1960). Her wisdom highly qualified her to explain the rapport between the camera and the actor. She believed in the psychic strength of the camera lens to capture what is going on inside of an actor. She also gave testimony to the power of a motion picture camera, which like an X-ray, has an uncanny facility to peer into an actor's interior. For the actor, the Inner Moving Object Exercise offers a rich inner substance that a camera is always eager to capture.

This exercise can offer an exciting adventure in acting technique as you sense your viscera surge with distinctively new energies. The result can be an increased sense of the pleasures in your inner space. Until recently the medical profession's access to internal organs depended on major invasive surgeries. Now doctors have the laparoscope, a video camera as tiny as 2 millimeters, that displays the innards of a patient and enables medical tests and procedures to be less complex. There is also a rotablator, a device like a small roto-rooter, which moves through the circulatory system of the body to clear clogged arteries. There is even a pill that has a camera in it which a person swallows enabling doctors to view the digestive tract.

You may want to consider the nature of these procedures as you use this exercise as a means of internal visualization to help you probe into your organs. Its purpose is to grant you a higher sensitization to inner qualities.

Stanislavski rebelled against the flailing of external parts with no inner reality. He developed means to create the inner reality experienced in the sensory exercises. The Inner Moving Object Exercise will enable you to contact force fields within and will invigorate you in a way far beyond the power of inner sensory exercises of sharp pain, sharp taste and sharp smell.

The therapeutic nature of this exercise creates a direct means of changing your internal functions. Scientific experiments have revealed that the electrical currents of the nervous system have a capacity for growth that is not fully appreciated. Experiments point out that the nervous system can grow new fibers; even the brain, as recently reported.

THE INNER MOVING OBJECT EXERCISE

1. Select an action.

2. Select an Inner Moving Object. The object can be as small as a thimble or coin, but preferably no larger than a tennis ball. It can also be a clump of energy—such as electricity—or it can be a ball of energy localized in the stomach to give it warmth. You can also miniaturize larger objects: animate objects such as a person or pet; inanimate objects such as telephones, musical instruments, or a compact disc player. The reason for miniaturizing an object, aside from the obvious aspect of it fitting, is so that you can carefully track its movement inside of you.

EXAMPLES

Action	Choice
To attain focus	Mechanical spring
To keep my secret	Cluster of spiders
To free myself	Flame of candle

Action	Choice
To shock them	Coiled rattlesnake
To share my power	Ice cube
To strike back	Door spring
To be in control of the situation	Diamond pin
To hold out	Circular saw
To have fun	Tape recorder

INNER MOVING OBJECT SUGGESTIONS

Light bulb	Teardrop
Cement pole	Tapeworm
Sexual part	Ulcer
Bubbles	Taffy
Barbed wire	Sugarcane chopper
Sharp object	Icicle
Needle	Fly
Merry-go-round	Greasy blob
Soggy cereal	Light beam
Erratic metronome	Razor blade
Lips	Glob of honey
Compression spring	Sandpaper

Fist

Fire

Soggy green moss

Molten lava

Cacti

Spinning top

Friendly pixie

Grandfather clock

Thorn

Opal

Amethyst

Red hot coal

Popping corn

Liquid ball of
   battery acid

Boxing gloves

Broken Glass

Compression springs

Brick

Radiating diamond

Baby rattle

Octopus

Scalpel

Magnetic bronze ball

Clump of rock music

Comet

Hot air balloon

Pinball

Ball bearing

Gong

Lover's heart

Orchid

Caterpillar

Spotlight

Ping-Pong ball

Caterpillar

Feather

Sea snail

White flame of truth

Guidelines for the Inner Moving Object Exercise

...Before allowing the object to move to different parts of your body, localize it in an area and define its shape. It can then move up and down inside of you—stopping, traveling a circuitous route, etc. Its routing will give rhythm and specific meaning to spoken words, phrases and sentences in improvisational or memorized dialogue.

...The object can be transformed into an amoeba-sized object, if you wish, and yet have the capacity to stretch, amorphously disintegrate and come together again.

...Taste it when it travels through the mouth; when it passes through the nose, smell it; hear it in the ears; treasure it in the heart (or maybe even let it break your heart); let it shake up deep recesses in the pelvic area.

...Let the object move into an area that resists it and then quickly expel it from that area. As you oust it, question the need for you to reroute the object.

...Use your choice to discover the nature of sensitivities in the nerve network. This exercise can also effectively deal with any locked areas, which often contain strong sensations. An object entering such a locked area can throw it open and create sensations with sudden spontaneity. So, if you have not successfully resolved locked-up areas, this exercise offers another opportunity.

...As a strong acting choice, I often describe the behavior that Jack Nicholson created in *One Flew Over the Cuckoo's Nest*. Perhaps you will vividly recall the scenes in which his character was subjected to electric shock therapy, his body writhing with the high voltage force of 10,000 volts that Nicholson imagined passing through his body. The Inner Moving Object is capable of creating such a force through an inventive and imaginative choice and your willingness to go with it.

I would like to relate a few of the unusual results I have seen students attain with this exercise:

An actor localized an object in his knees where he had pain for several days. His choice of a cluster of electrical energy totally relieved the pain. After completing the exercise, he showed an exuberance I had never seen as he realized that he could actually change, at will, bodily feelings and sensations.

An actress created a wider vocal range for the first time when she did the exercise. It took months of previous sensorial and early superconscious exercises to reach this achievement.

An actress used an Inner Moving Object of a heart in her head area, and the expressions seen on her face captured the lively pulsations of a pumping heart.

An actor used a large gold nugget in his solar plexus. Its use became like a solar plexus energy that sent forth white light into the body.

After you have gained assurance in working with a single object to ignite interior energies, you can then select two objects.

EXAMPLES

Action	Choices
To get on the good side	Diamond in head area Bubble in stomach
To mock everyone	Fly in head Moving ulcer in stomach
To bewitch	Phosphorescent indigo blob Seashell
To shock them	Buzzing chain saw in head Razor blade traveling through muscle tissues
To guide	Spinning top in head Comet in veins
To make them laugh	Aluminum foil in head 4th of July sparkler
To know no boundaries	Roman God Mercury I Ching hexagram
To pester	Violin bow Glob of molasses
To prepare the earth	Ice cube in head Fireball - Lower part of body

You can also select one or two objects to use in combination with another choice.

EXAMPLES OF THE INNER MOVING
OBJECT COMBINATION EXERCISE

Action	Choices
To rip open delicate matters	IMO - Spouting geyser Diamond Introjection
To emancipate	IMO - Small prayer scroll Sp.Obj. - Outer space creatures
To carry out an important mission	IMO - Electric coil current in torso Warm ball in throat Sex object in chest Cement poles in legs Sp. Obj. - Hands touching me
To protect my dignity	IMO - Ice cube in head Ch.Imp. - Electricity in groin to spinal area

OUTER SPATIAL OBJECTS EXERCISE

Prayer, chanting, ESP, remote viewing and harmonic convergence are forms of concentration related to vibrations that can be transmitted toward intimate or distant points. Tibetan spiritual healers can, after a particular type of concentration, touch their patients and permit energies to enter into afflicted areas. Eastern disciplines emphasize the use of energy sources within the body, such as chakras, which enable one to make contact with higher and more human levels of consciousness and away from the animal instincts of a lower level.

During his period of yogic studies, Stanislavski evolved a prana ray emission exercise. Prana energy is often described as having powers of healing radiation, frequencies and electrical transmissions. Stanislavski's interest in ray emissions illustrates the spiritual growth principles inherent in his thought. In the exercise, he had actors sit in a circle and transmit energy to one another without words or sounds. Its purpose was to strengthen inner spiritual values between actors and in relation to their environment. Today, many engage in pranayama, a rhythmic breathing exercise, as a gateway to higher consciousness.

The Outer Spatial Objects Exercise represents a new stage of development. More than the previous superconscious exercises, it seeks interconnections with potential human powers—the very same kind of powers Stanislavski attempted to develop in his ray emission experiments. This exercise has the same purpose as Stanislavski's experiment: to enrich communication between you and your performance environment of actors, scenery, camera and audience. Its intention is to help you discover and refine your possession of this human potential. It offers an intriguing exploratory process during which you gain greater insight into your own hidden energies. It advances your progress toward a more effective and expressive acting instrument. The exercise offers you a refined way of becoming aware of your unexplored creative resources and enhances your ability to intelligently gauge their power.

Your body houses electrical force which you can transmit by the use of your conscious will; this exercise grants you more conscious control of your instrumental energies. You will quickly discover rich acting subtleties as you transmit hidden energies to create rhythmic frequencies and spatial dimensions. The exercise seeks to have you experience a different kind of connectedness with the acting space you inhabit and in the process, discover your ability to transmit energy waves with minimal vocal and physical values—a highly desirable ability for creating natural acting energies. The Outer Spatial Objects Exercise connects you with your acting space as you radiate energies from within you into the environment that encompasses you.

It is an ideal exercise for dealing with any degree of stage fright. Even if you find yourself battling with bouts of stage fright, realize that even Laurence Olivier struggled with the same fear. Through your conscious will, you can effect a cure for stage fright by emitting energies which touch the audience and camera rather than allowing the energies of the audience and camera to touch you. Stage fright chiefly occurs when you sense disheartening, negative energy from the force field that surrounds you.

In my workshop, I have seen actors gain an improved physical tone and presence when exploring this exercise. With remarkable consistency, the flow of energies from an actor's instrument results in increased physical prowess and effortless acting. These energy-charged emissions produce an exceptionally rich chemistry.

Body energies can even be detected in statues, paintings and drawings. Michelangelo's drawings depict various parts of the human anatomy such as the arms, hands, sometimes a thumb, muscles of the biceps, thighs, calves, etc. A study of his drawings can be helpful in noting the definition and energy in one part of the body while the rest of the body is faintly sketched.

Examples of the relationship between inner energies and physical accomplishments are plentiful in the world of outstanding athletes and artists. Recall a sight you may have witnessed of a spectacular cross-court throw, when the ball arcs perfectly into the basket and think about it in terms of the basketball player's ability to concentrate inner energies on that distant target. Similarly, a Zen archer can guide the arrow to the center of a target—even with both eyes closed! You can probably also think of supreme ballet dancers who let energy out through their toes when they stretch their legs. The Outer Spatial Objects Exercise attempts to stimulate these uses of inner energies.

Some philosophies and disciplines focus on lifting energies from the base of the spine and permitting them to travel up the spine to the point located at the center of the top of the head. The energy is then released into the force field existing in the sphere above the head. Some have found personal benefit in ridding the brain of unwanted thoughts by banishing them into the outer sphere above the head.

As a creative researcher, I have relied on behavioral results to verify the creative usefulness of an exercise. With the Outer Spatial Objects Exercise, I have witnessed outcomes which were astonishing.

One of the most extraordinary results happened when an actor chose to radiate energy from his eyes. His exploration of this exercise brought me to the edge of my chair, with my mouth agape in wonderment, as I beheld him emitting white beams from his eyes. I had to tell myself that I was not hallucinating but rather was witnessing a phenomenon. I was deeply grateful that the actor had given me the hidden truth of the exercise, just as the truth of other exercises has been revealed to me in startling ways by actors apparently already in tune with higher levels of human abilities.

Using energy from the heart and testicles, an actor created an unusual combination of sensual and sexual feelings.

Another actor, who admitted having tendencies to think more than to feel, achieved an increased physical tone by releasing energies from his hips and mouth. He created a palpable, but graceful presence as he was drawn gently in the direction of the energies emanating from his chosen areas.

Chet Walker, who belongs to the Basketball Hall of Fame, studied with me for a year before going into film production. His gentle and sensitive nature was extremely heightened during his use of Outer Spatial Objects. For this exercise, he used the same concentrational power he had projected into basketballs so many times before when playing on court. Later, his acting began to assume the dramatic stature of Paul Robeson.

An actor attempting to develop his chest resonance was able to emit strong resonant waves from his chest area.

An international dancer discovered the telepathic properties of this exercise during an incident when she had scolded her teenage son for having removed the patina from a 400 year-old Buddha statue she had recently acquired. The son thought she would like it better if it were "cleaned up," and had hoped to surprise her with its shiny new look. She was so angry that she told him that she never wanted to see the statue again. Stricken with remorse, her son retreated to his room. In her own room, she began to feel regret for her behavior toward her son. She began to radiate parts of herself through the large house and into his room, visualizing her energy soothing her son. A little later, when they saw each other again, her son remarked that he sensed an energy enter into his room and was extremely comforted. Through this exercise she had discovered her own hidden force to heal, as others have discovered such powers through prayer, chanting and meditation.

Some of my early co-explorers achieved the following results:

Choice	Result
Hands - cheeks	A romantic tenderness not previously expressed.
Lips - breasts - crotch	An actress created an unusual free-flowing movement.
Arms - chest	An actor created extremely interesting behavior with his partner in an improvisation. He created the illusion of physical contact.
Arms	A tall actor experienced a different physical sense. His classmates remarked that he was less self-conscious about his height.
Nose - teeth	An actress achieved an exceptionally centered strength and belief.
Network of veins	The actor entangled his partner in an imaginary net.

An actor developed an unusual sense of a clone of himself in the space around him. The experience endowed him with an increased consciousness of his entire acting instrument.

THE OUTER SPATIAL OBJECTS EXERCISE

1. Select an action that you feel is particularly applicable for the nature of this exercise.

2. Select a choice or choices from the suggestion list that will fulfill your action's meaning:

EXAMPLES

Action	Choices
To go with the flow	Eyes - lips - knees
To blunder	Lips - elbows - base of spine - knees
To demand recognition	Sexual organs - chest

CHOICE SUGGESTIONS

Pelvis - breasts

Hips - pectoral muscles - legs

Collarbone

Lower half of body

Mouth - back - hips

Dandruff flakes

Thighs - chest

Back - hip area

Eyes - feet - mouth

Dimples - nipples

Nerve network of body

Eyelashes

Right Foot - teeth

Thighs - feet - hands

Lips

Spine

Feet - right arm

Crotch - breasts

Arms - eyes

Ears

Arms - chest

Chest - mouth

Hips - breasts

Pelvis - breast

Jaw - elbows - knees

Eyeballs - hands

Feet - thighs

Pores scented
   with Jasmine oil

Intestines

Anus - lips

Erect penis - eyes

Stinky feet and armpits

Center of chest - knees

Throat - thumbnails

Hands - fingers

Eyebrows - jaw - shoulders

Lips - bust - crotch

Torso - leg network

Mouth - chin - cheeks

Hands - cheeks

Eyes - hands - mouth

Legs - solar plexus

Right ear - left nostril

Heart - arms

Lungs

Clitoris - breasts

Navel - legs - eyelashes

Pubic hair

Lower abdomen - forehead

Sexual center - heart

Guidelines for the
Outer Spatial Objects Exercise

...Create energetic sensations in the area(s) chosen or sense the basic energy in the area(s). Define the energy as hot, warm, cold, strong, weak, etc.

...When this exercise is done following a period of relaxation, the body is ready to permit energy to flow effortlessly. Sense yourself sending forth natural radiations and body frequencies—powerful faculties possessed by all fine performers. It will be revelatory when you experience the release of energies from unaccustomed areas. Permit the sensation to exist without activating any muscles in the chosen area(s).

...With a relaxed but energized feeling in the chosen area(s), you can more easily sense the energy of body parts drift into surrounding spaces. Use imaginative control in the manner in which you modulate the flow and stream— quickly, slowly, gradually, in spurts, etc. The controlling element should have relevance to the behavior you wish to create for your action.

...It is important that you not move the chosen area(s). You cannot physically send parts of your body into nearby or distant areas, but you can propel energy waves from those specified parts. The body should be motionless as you effortlessly release the energy. Fulfill your intention not in a physically overt way, but with silently transmitted energies.

...While sitting or standing, project the energy into a nearby area and then gradually into farther areas. The energy flow of the exercise is not exclusively a frontal flow. If you are using the spine as a choice, propel the spine's energy into the space behind you. For example, an actress who permitted the energy of her eyes to go out through the back of her head remarked on the unusual kind of dimensional experience it created.

...Allow the energy of your chosen area(s) to be released in regular or irregular waves and patterns. The projection of energies can have different designs: a missile on course, zigzagged patterns, explosive bubbles, soft streams of feeling or uncontrollable frequencies. Consciously will the transference of these types of energies while maintaining contact with the areas which generate and control the energy flow.

...Connect with the force field around you when you walk. Sense the energy ahead of you and drawing you towards the object of your attention, whether it is a person or another part of the environment. There is a strong belief in scientific circles that the atoms which passed through every person who has ever lived on this earth are the same atoms that currently pass through all of us. It is believed that each of us breathes in air molecules that were once breathed in and exhaled by past humans including Aristotle, Gandhi, Newton, etc. This phenomenon creates a universal connection of humankind.

This exercise enables actors to cultivate a sense of being able to penetrate the performance space shared with other actors and create the much-desired value known as ensemble acting.

Examples of the Outer Spatial Objects Combination Exercise

To beguile
OSO - Lips - neck - abdomen
Sp. Obj. - Moonbeams

To inspire
OSO - Eyes - chest - thighs - soles of feet
    Ch.Imp. - Enthusiasm.
        OA: Intense heat in genitals
        DA: Throat

To get someone in bed
OSO - Eyes - breasts - crotch
    Sp. Obj. - Water jets from a waterfall

To challenge
OSO - Center of forehead, eyes, hands
    Ch. Imp. - Anger
        OA: Pounding in brain
        DA: Stomach

To regain my masculinity
OSO - Heart extended out of chest
Ch.Imp. - Warmth
        OA: Solar plexus
        DA: - Arms and legs

To castigate
OSO - Heart
    Sp. Obj. - Pounding fists

To flirt
OSO - Eyes
    Ch. Imp. - Tenderness.
        OA: Warmth in base of spine
        DA: Base of head

To have a ball
OSO - Intestines
    Ch. Imp. - Joy
        OA: Head
        DA: Legs

To worm out of trouble
OSO - Forehead - eyes - shoulders
    IMO - Electric sparks in arms and fingers

To speak outright
OSO - Hands - tongue - lips
    Introjection of a person

PHYSIOLOGICAL AND PSYCHOLOGICAL EXERCISE

In ancient physiology, various body parts were seen to possess their own independent psyches, emotions and meanings. Oscar Ichazo of The Arica Institute updated this ancient doctrine by synthesizing beliefs of the Ancient Greeks, Hinduism, Buddhism, Sufism, and the tenets of the Russian mystic, George Gurdjieff. Ichazo's "updated doctrine" inspired this exercise.

The Physiological and Psychological Exercise can be your personal trainer, giving attention to specific body areas until a desired presence is achieved. It will require you to investigate and define your senses, organs and anatomical parts to shape the physiological and psychological aspects of your own personal presence or that of a character. When applying this exercise, I have seen actors achieve remarkably new physical sensibilities, magically nuanced responses and more impassioned feelings.

This exercise enables the actor to communicate enormous inner power with any part of the body. The results enhance both inner inclinations and outer kinetic energy. The kinetic energy can be harmonious or competitive, e.g., the heart confluent with or versus the head.

One actor in my workshop reacted to readings about the exercise by suggesting that it seemed to be a repetition of sensory work in which he had been thoroughly trained. I suggested that he take a stab at it anyway. We both acknowledged that the results of his first attempt were greater poise and an infinitely superior inner and outer expressiveness. The way he had employed sensory choices seemed to elicit conventionalities when compared to the unique and lively details that he attained working with this superconscious exercise. Though he did not abandon the use of sensory choices, he discovered that he could use his training in a more imaginative and effective way. As he had been a pre-med student, he said the nature of the exercise may have awakened his understanding of the connections between the body and the physiological aspects of his acting instrument. He also discovered, as do all who do the exercise, that organs other than the sensory organs abound with their own special communicative powers.

This exercise can be used alone or in combination with other tools. The examples will convey how certain choices create behavioral nuances by developing, simultaneously, inner emotions and a new outer physical tone.

Now and then, I have seen the exercise offer tremendous value changes to an actor who, for whatever reason, has not been able to achieve a well-sharpened acting image through sensory choices. The following is an example of the choices and results in the work of a developing actor as he gave each body organ the respective physiological and psychological values.

Action: To doubt their faithfulness
Eyes: To see the world of epistles
Ears: To hear them speak of one's virtues
Mouth and stomach: To hunger for more sensitivity

Heart: To pump freedom through my veins
Thighs and arms: To hold up under the lies

The resulting battle between his outer physiological choices and inner psychological created an immensely interesting physical presence, a goal upon which we had been concentrating. The duality of his choices both drained and energized him. He also created an enormously rich emotional disturbance as powerful as a successful Emotional Memory exercise might elicit but infinitely more artistic. One of the most expressive results was the holding back of tears welling up in his eyes.

The second time he did the exercise, he used the following:

Action: To figure it out
Ears: To hear gibberish
Eyes: To see everything in motion
Genitals: To feel isolation and dislike
Hands and feet: To reach out for compassion

The genital choice created intense inner pain and the gestures of his hands and feet were both introverted and outgoing. These expressive results were accompanied by stirring, sensitive emotions which contained sparks of anger.

The third time, he did the exercise in combination with other exercise choices.

Action: To pull myself together
Eyes: To see miles down the road

Ears: To hear approaching horses
  Ch. Imp. - Courage
    OA: Heart
    DA: Shoulders and arms

(He also added the quality of narcissism to his character by using the sensory choices of smell for the head area and sun on the legs.)

This actor was able to create an energetic style that he had never achieved before and which attested to his ability to work with classical material. His energy in the exercise combined a physical forward thrust with disorganized features. In addition, flashes of danger occurred in a cold but playful manner.

This talented actor discovered that the Physiological and Psychological Exercise can be an intellectual and artistic pursuit as manifested in his choices and results. It catapulted his work into another dimension and he attained a higher level of expressive freedom.

I have seen other examples of the splendid values that come to fruition with this exercise. I vividly recall how an extremely well-trained and experienced actor achieved a vocal quality resonating fierce sound waves that had previously eluded him. Another actor, who never seemed at ease with his height, was able to create a fluidity from his feet to his head. This was an "open sesame" moment creating a doorway to progress that enabled him to fulfill ensuing exercises with more skill.

Guidelines for the Physiological and Psychological Exercise

...Above all, you must have complete and total faith in its possibilities for you. This exercise examines the situation and life perspective of a character. It will enable you to discover the consciousness and functioning which independently exist in a character's various body areas. In this process, you may even find areas that your acting instrument has heretofore used only in a vague way.

...Put your consciousness into different areas. For example, do not consciously think about where to put your feet; with a choice for that area your consciousness is in your feet, and therefore the choice will guide feet movement and placement.

...Develop a sense of when you are on target with your choices so that you quickly become aware of when one of the choices goes off center.

...As part of your film technique, you can plan choices for the camera to capture your personal chemistry, particularly as reflected in your facial expressions.

...With your choices you can increase the range of your physical presence with knowledge of this new technique to generate palpable images.

...When you freely change your focus from one choice to another, you may discover a fresh kind of spontaneity in your work. This is sometimes experienced when you permit the choices, as in any combination, to compete against each other as they vie for supremacy.

In using inner organs to communicate your actions, keep in mind that they have both spiritual and physical values.

The following list is taken from an interview between Sam Keen and Oscar Ichazo of the Arica Institute:

Ears perceive the meaning or logos and give us substance of things.

Eyes isolate forms.

The nose smells out possibilities.

The mouth and stomach sense our needs for nourishment.

The heart energizes the organism with its impulse.

The liver assimilates food and percepts we take into the organism.

The colon, anus, bladder and kidneys eliminate foods, ideas and experiences that are unmetabolizable.

The genitals reflect our orientation toward or away from life.

The thighs and upper arms reflect our capacity or strength.

The knees and elbows reflect the ease or awkwardness, the charisma with which we move through the world.

The calves and forearms are the means we use.

The hands and feet are used for going and taking, for reaching out for goals.

With my students, I have expanded the Arica Institute choices so that the exercise would be more useful for an actor's training. The following are choices made by my students:

EXAMPLES

To heal
Eyes: For soul searching
Heart: To feel
Hands and arms: To touch and hold true values
Feet and legs: To carry out a mission

To haul over the coals
Mouth: To savor the pain
Heart: To energize the anger
Stomach: To feel the guilt
Legs and feet: To reach my prey

To let it out
Eyes: To see the wonders of the world
Heart: To give energy
Hands and feet: To reach for fun things

To fantasize
Arms and hands: To exalt a dream
Heart: To traverse exotic lands
Genitals: To relish caresses

To free myself from guilt
Ears: To hear negativity
Eyes: To seek reassurance
Thighs: To hide
Stomach and mouth: To release guilt

To tantalize
Ears: To hear dirty language
Nose: To smell out the possibilities
Heart: To glue courage
Thighs: To hide
Feet: To limit action

To be the devil's advocate
Eyes: To pierce
Ears: To hear both sides
Mouth: To express confidence
Bowels: To eliminate unnecessary ideas
Feet and legs: To stand my ground

To rejoice
Eyes: To see joyful things
Ears: To hear exuberant sounds
Heart: For energizing the body
Knees and elbows: For spontaneous expression

To cast off mediocrity
Mouth and throat: To taste forbidden potions
Spine: To absorb ocean waves
Hands: To shed drab colors
Feet: To avoid the mire

To get someone in bed
Eyes: To see sexual acts
Mouth: To taste sweets
Genitals: To fuel sexual excitement

To give myself
Eyes: To see auras
Nose: To smell the auras
Ears: To hear the illusion
Mouth and digestive system: To eat nectar
Hair: To sense energy

To avenge myself on them all
Eyes: To see the horror
Ears: To hear discordant crying and screaming
Mouth: To taste bitterness
Nose: To smell out possibilities to do harm

To involve them in my experience
Ears: To hear a celebration
Eyes: To see the truth
Heart: To give power to the universe
Genitals: For frustration
Knees and elbows: For confidence

To reach my center
Spine: To hold it all together
Soles of feet: To connect with the earth
Eyes: As barriers to the soul
Throat: For expression

To please the world
Eyes: To search for kindness
Mouth and stomach: To sense disapproval
Hands: To show my affection and love

To live it up
Hair: To attract electricity
Ears: To hear laughter and sound of champagne glasses
Eyes: To see what I have never seen before
Thighs: To jump hurtles

To degrade
Eyes: To scrutinize pieces of pseudo-art
Body: To absorb distasteful elements
Hands: To take away their egos
Thighs and legs: To assert my stature
Nose: To smell their shortcomings

To run away
Ears: To hear the cries of sorrow
Eyes: To see the tyrants
Thighs and upper arms: To embrace and protect

To be on guard
Eyes: To isolate the truth
Ears: To hear positive sounds
Nose: To smell out good and bad possibilities
Stomach: To digest glass

To set on fire
Eyes: To see pornographic pictures
Nose: To smell out possibilities
Hands and feet: To carry forth opportunity
Genitals: To forge forward

To release my anger
Feet: To stand for what I am
Hands: To push and grab
Eyes: To see the truth
Stomach: To digest goodness and regurgitate poison

To make them acknowledge my presence
Hands: To create
Legs: To take me where I want to go
Smile: To mask insecurities

To find out the secret
Ears: To translate meanings
Eyes: To identify the center
Liver: To filter poisons
Thighs and upper arms: To maintain strength

To accuse
Eyes: To see their souls
Ears: To hear the lies
Heart: To pump the power
Arms: To keep them at a distance

To escape great danger
Ears: To pick up vibrations
Nose: To smell danger
Skin: To repel energy
Breath: To make me invisible
Genitals: To hold the possibility of life
Thighs and upper arms: To gather strength

To dominate everything
Eyes: To see things in miniature
Mouth: To taste control
Ears: To hear praise
Hands: To reach out and possess

The following choices were selected by Madeleine Thornton-Sherwood, a notable member of The Actors Studio during its formative years and long thereafter. When I told her that all of her choices were fulfilled except the one for her knees, she agreed. It was almost as if she had been challenging the exercise. The fact that we both agreed that of all her choices the one in the knees was the weakest evinced, confirmed for her the merit of the exercise in conveying acting energies.

To remain true to myself
Eyes: To see cars moving
Nose: To smell good aromas
Mouth: To chew soft food, soft words, soft friends
Ears: To hear the silence of the dead
Heart: To energize my energies
Stomach: To reject food and accept liquid
Genitals: To desire and desist
Knees: For easy movement
Feet and hands: For reaching out and going forth

PHYSIOLOGICAL AND PSYCHOLOGICAL COMBINATION EXAMPLES

To prepare myself for love
Eyes: To see the good side
Hands: To touch the soul
Skin: To be tantalized
Stomach: To sense danger

To nurture those around me
Hands: Reaching out to comfort others
Liver: To absorb unpleasant experiences of others
Colon and bladder: To eliminate those experiences
Ch. Imp. - Love.
    OA: - Warm syrup in heart
    DA: - Head

To force a connection
Nose: To smell out trouble
Elbows and knees: For charisma
Body: To absorb distasteful things
OSO - Eyes

To pierce and captivate the universe
Eyes: For penetration
Arms: For expression
Mouth: To entice
OSO - Legs

To guide
Heart: To pump the necessary stream of life
Thighs and upper arms: For the gift of life energy
Genitals: For enjoyment
Sp. Obj. - Sacred tablets

To rouse
Eyes: To perceive raging fire
Ears: To hear an intense driving sound
Mouth and stomach: To perceive hunger

Genitals: To sense pleasure
Feet: To make the earth tremble and to go after goals
OSO - Eyes vibrating out through center of forehead

To flush them out
Eyes: To detect weakness or flaws
Body: To send out energy to them
Taste: Blood
IMO - Straight razor in digestive tract

To rid myself of guilt
Eyes and ears: To see and hear cosmic realities
Heart: To pump the necessary stream of life
Introjection

To share my secret
Eyes: To see closed places
Ears: To hear a new sound
Nose: To sniff an opportunity
Heart: To give energy
Genitals: To fear rejection
Ch. Imp. - Nervousness.
    OA: - Queasiness in stomach
    DA: - Eyes

AURA EXERCISE

The first time someone mentioned the aura you emanate, you may have replied, "What are you talking about?" Even now, if someone inquires about your auras, you may have no choice but to answer "I haven't the vaguest idea." This exercise will acquaint you with your auric presence and guide you in creating a character's aura. During the process of discovering character auras, you will discover that auras radiate from within as a part of your natural chemistry, and you will become more acquainted with the auric qualities which convey your persona.

Numerous times, during my years of study with the American Stanislavski disciples, I heard of their adoration of Eleanora Duse whom Stanislavski also adored and was one of the actors who inspired his System.

They gave detailed descriptions of her performances, but for some reason I do not recall any mention of the phenomenon that some members of her audiences witnessed in the performances she gave during the last years of her life. It seemed to them as if she had created a "misty light" on stage. This was just one manifestation of the uncanny gifts that enabled her to create the mystical in acting. Another such gift was the power to speak in a whisper, yet be audible in the farthest reaches of a theater.

The acceptance of concepts and ideas often depends upon whether they are scientifically provable. Sometimes even when scientific proof has been established, doubt can still linger.

Scientists, while weeding out the charlatans, have confirmed the abilities of gifted clairvoyants to see auric colors around people. Among such scientists are those who have used Kirlian photography at UCLA and established that roses, lizards, rocks, leaves, coins and a host of other objects—even the human body—radiate colors. Perhaps, you have seen the stunning Kirlian photographs of auras radiating from hands. Swami Muktananda (who had conversations with astronaut Edgar Mitchell about his spiritual experience on the moon) after some persuasion by a Kirlian photographer, agreed to have one of his fingers photographed. What the photograph revealed was a halo of brilliant rays. Similarly, other researchers have seen pure colors captured on film when photographing the fingertips of healers. Some have even suggested that the auric field that surrounds a medical doctor gives benefit to the patient, and others have suggested that the doctor's aura may accomplish an actual cure. Yogis will point out that we can pass the energy of our chakras to another. This is the kind of communication that Stanislavski was investigating in his yogic prana ray emission experiments with actors.

The Los Angeles Times reported that a survey revealed that 47% of the journalism students at Columbia University believed in aura readings. It is appropriate for student journalists to believe in the reading of auras, since journalists are often required to put into words what they feel vibrates from the people they encounter in search of a story. Positive features can be a warm disposition, a radiant smile, glistening eyes or an electrical presence. Negative personalities can convey dark colors, icy eyes or "vibes" that can give one the creeps. All of these qualities can be translated into colors. The actor, can consciously or unconsciously store such features in the memory for future characterization values.

Stanislavski experimented with an electrical spinning wheel affixed with various colored light bulbs. He wanted to discover if actors could be emotionally affected by the spinning wheel of colors. In the final years of developing his System, his early experiments with lights were refined. At that time, he was exploring how the boldness or weakness of a color could relate to the energy of the physical activity of a character in a scene.

Practitioners of holistic health apparently believe that colors do serve a purpose in healing. They have developed specific methods for breathing in colors to benefit both mind and body, e.g., green to purify the blood; deep rose to be in harmony with others; light blue for insomnia, etc. Such a process is not much different from that used by some of Stanislavski's American adherents to arouse organic emotions through the value of colors.

I have always given attention to which superconscious exercises my students favor for creating behavioral values. Students seem to gravitate toward the Aura Exercise, revealing what is perhaps a natural instinct in actors to want to capture the energies present in life and art. A richly talented actor will radiate energetic colors; less expressive colors will be present in an actor lacking dramatic energy.

A brief description of color values is followed by exercise examples which will discuss further the colors that can be used to capture the meanings of actions and character types.

COLOR VALUES

WHITE: Purity, unity, high spiritual devotion, ecstasy.

PURPLE: Power, greatness, honor, respect.

VIOLET: Holiness, humility, reverence, sublimity, beauty, high spirituality, healing, art, mysticism.

BLUE: Truth, peace, faith, religious worship, meditation, loyalty.

INDIGO: Intelligence, integrity.

YELLOW: Intellectual search, self discipline, desire for knowledge, laughter, optimistic.

GOLD: High spiritual calmness.

PINK: Sympathy, compassion, love, gentleness, sincerity, kindness, refinement.

ORANGE:	Intelligence, learning, assurance, self-confidence, balance.
RED:	Strength, respect, power, vitality, love.
GREEN:	Energy, hope, balance, youth, health, success, pride.
INDIGO:	Mystery, deep concentration, self-understanding.
LAVENDER:	High spirituality.

The preceding list are colors associated with virtues. Some darker colors tend to reveal negativity.

BROWN:	Avarice
BLACK:	Depraved
DARK GREEN:	Jealousy
OLIVE:	Deceit
DARK YELLOW:	Suspicion
CLOUDY RED:	Greed

Guidelines for the Aura Exercise

...Decide upon your action and, as with any new exercise, formulate an action that can lead you into more daring areas. During a scene, auras can assume new currents, just as colors can change in hue and intensity as the light shifts or the visual context alters.

...Think of the exercise as another opportunity for you to give more meaning to the space that surrounds you. A prime concern in your experimentation with this exercise should be the illumination of the space around you. This is a quality for which any performer should strive. The exercise can offer you the means to grant a palpability to the space you illuminate. Early in his career, the rock star Sting is said to have developed a visceral aura which intimidated and even frightened people. Later, the threatening nature of his aura greatly diminished when he began to align himself with humanitarian concerns.

...During the exercise, try to maneuver and guide your auric energy. Verify that you are not a hit-or-miss actor, but can be right on target with the energy you emit. Believe that your acting instrument can create auric energies with a mysteriously powerful vitality. Sometimes the vitality of a person is so strong that we mysteriously sense the person's aura even after his or her departure from a room or place. You can leave a lasting impression with casting directors by stimulating inner and outer colors.

...A highly refined type of concentration can be developed in this exercise as you surround yourself with a light which nothing can disturb. You develop a glowing, relaxed presence in any professional or personal situation. Manipulation of the aura is another way of enhancing your presence for communication with a receptive audience or of protecting yourself against disruptive elements in a hostile environment.

...Some have postulated that our auric energy extends an inch beyond our bodies and provides us with a private place. Others feel that our auric energy can radiate for a distance of up to 24 inches from our bodies. In film acting, the exercise can be helpful in creating expressive behavior within the confines of close-up shots.

...Since particular colors are associated with the inner organs, you can internalize a color with the use of choices for certain areas. A sense of burning red, fiery coals in the solar plexus can create a simmering inner aura, which can be maneuvered into a Channeling Impulse. You can also permit an aura to stream outward as an Outer Spatial Object.

...Invent colors for yourself; colors that you may not think exist in you. In creating a character, Olivier said that he painted portraits of the character in his mind.

EXAMPLES

To let it all out
Lemon yellow - Heart
Deep rose pink - Eyes
Golden rays - Around irises
Emerald green - Body

To infuse them with love
Pink - Body
White - Hands
Blue/Yellow - Torso

To reveal my muscular power
Red - Muscular system
Burnt umber - Genitals
Silver - Eyes and tongue

To go one step further
Indigo - Head
Green - Body
Dark yellow - Stomach

To probe
Yellow - Head
Dark green - Face
Green - Chest
Red - Arms, legs and crotch

To fight for my way
Black - Head
Red - Heart
Green - Crotch

To speak from my heart to their souls
Lavender - Eyes
Violet and gold - Heart and chest
Red and black clouds - Stomach

To push a hidden agenda
Magenta and gold shades - Throat and head
Black - Eyes
Olive - Heart

To satisfy my anger
Red - Eyes, arms, fingers and toes
Black - Mouth and pelvis

To awaken
Green - Knees and elbows
White - Fingers and toes

To worm out of trouble
Olive green - Knees, elbows, fingers
                and toes
Dark green - Mouth
Deep scarlet - Eyes

To make a connection
Violet - Torso and heart
Gold - Shoulders, head, arms, wrists and hands

To stand above everyone
Orange - Head
Red - Crotch
Green - Upper and lower body

To realize the Buddha in myself
Purple - Entire body
Blue - Stomach

To keep my eyes open
Pink - Heart
Indigo - Skin and hair

To never give an inch
Purple - Eyes and nose
Green - Chest and back
Red - Arms and legs

To save my soul
Murky orange - Heart, eyes, feet and voice

To be scary
Shades of red - Heart, brain and lymph
                glands

To be a loon
Silver - Base of spine
Green - Spleen, hands and feet

To feel good about what I'm doing
Purple - Nervous system
Blue - Lungs and eyes
Yellow - Muscles

To seduce
Shades of red and black - Reproductive organs
Crimson - Eyes and mouth
Scarlet - Remainder of body

To enjoy my surroundings
Blue - Solar plexus
Violet - Brain
Yellow - Legs

To haul over the coals
White - Head
Dark blue - Eyes
Burnt orange - Chest

To enlighten
Lavender - Eyes
Green - Lungs
Red - Abdomen

To seek comfort
Yellow - Brain
Pink - Heart
Red - Lungs
Silver - Toes and fingers
Green - Reproductive organs

To get back to a better time
Silver - Thyroid gland
Deep crimson speckled with black - Heart

To break their will
Black - Head
Red - Eyes
Cool green - Hands
Blue - Legs

To draw the line
Orange - Head
Green - Arms

To win
White - Crown chakra
Green - Heart chakra

EXAMPLES OF AURA COMBINATION EXERCISE

To keep going
Blue - Face
Gold - Hair
Ch. Imp. - Laughter
   OA: Throat
   DA: Hands and fingers
IMO - Willow branches down spine and into arms

To know the difference
Orange - Skin
Pink - Skeleton
IMO - Laser beams

To pick up the pieces
Yellow - Mouth
Sea blue - Breasts
Gray - Toes and feet
Black - Skin and hair
Ch. Imp. - Tightness
    OA: Temples
    DA: Eyes

To swim against
Pink - Upper body
Green - Lower body
Sp. Obj. - Spitballs

To stir up the moment
Red and orange - Head
Yellow - Body
IMO - Electrical coil

To proceed boldly
Blue - Head and arms
Green - Body and legs
P & P - Mouth to speak my mind
       Eyes to see the light

To burn my bridges
Crimson - Solar plexus
P & P - Eyes to see violence in movies
       Mouth to cultivate distaste

To needle
Fire truck red - Legs
Gold - Brain
Sp. Obj. - Massaging hands on upper body

To arrive at the last stop
Silver - Skeletal system
Green - Respiratory system
OSO - Eyes and extremities

To reveal a secret
White - Face and heart
Green - Body
OSO - Cheekbones and mouth

To remain on my feet
Yellow - Head
Purple - Torso and legs
Green - Arms and hands

To play it cool
Pale blue - Eyes
Gold - Hands
IMO - Glass fragments
Sp. Obj. - Popping hot grease

To play with them
Green - Spleen
IMO - Ice Cube

To be confused
Pink - Head and heart
Green - Body
Sp. Obj. - Ropes

To reproach
Gold - Reproductive organs
Red - Heart
P&P - Hands to stroke the ego
P&P - Eyes to pierce

To get lost in my sexual fantasies
Black - Entire body
Sp. Obj. - Feathers on face
Sp. Obj. - Snakes up and down body

To keep attached to people
Red and Orange - Torso and arms
Sp. Obj. - Electromagnetic field
Ch. Imp. - Electric bursts from
           pineal gland to legs

To draw the line
Blue - Entire body
P&P - Elbows to insure my space
     Lungs to assess my situation
OSO - Hands

PROJECTED SPATIAL OBJECT

One concern in preparing a role lies in entering into the spirit of the locale in which a character dwells. To understand the locale of a character, some actors will travel great distances for the purpose of soaking up the actual atmosphere of a character's habitat, environment and surroundings. If a movie is to be an "on-location shoot," an actor might journey to a film location before shooting begins in order to live and immerse oneself in the character's physical world. However, if the geographical place of a story is recreated on a set inside a film studio or on a studio's outdoor backlot, the actor who seeks more than only absorbing copied, sterile environs has two options: to visit the actual geographical place (if time and funds permit), or, to tap into other resources such as photographs, paintings or videos of the actual locale. Besides the development of a more enhanced characterization, the rewards of such creative research can include a deeper interest and appreciation in art, sculpture, anthropology and culture.

This exercise, unlike the introjection exercise, arouses an interest in creating a role not only by studying people of a certain region for their traits and mannerisms, but also by living in a character's habitat. From the effective results I have witnessed, I have always considered the Projected Spatial Object exercise a highly refined development of the basic Method exercise of Creating a Place.

Psychiatrist Carl Jung, whom many feel laid

the foundation for New Age thought, had a mystical connection with material objects. While discussing poltergeists during one of his meetings with Sigmund Freud, he told Freud that a large cupboard would momentarily let out a cracking noise. When it actually did, Freud turned white. That may have been the beginning of Freud's gradual change in his beliefs about the psychic world. On another occasion, during talks with his longtime friend Lauren van der Post, Jung warned about a recording machine with which van der Post had hoped to record Jung's spontaneous thoughts. Jung believed recording machines harbored animosity towards him and even if inanimate, could still be hostile. Jung's intuition went unheeded and nearly seventy hours of recording were damaged and lost forever. Jung had a strong belief that both animate and inanimate objects, as well as human beings, are joined through his famous theory of the collective unconscious.

In Yosemite, John Muir could spend an entire day studying a plant unknown to him. With each new plant he attempted to establish an intimate interconnection as a revealing source of insight about the species.

In the planetary village of Findhorn on the northern coast of Scotland, not far from the Arctic Circle, the residents have a strong belief in the spirits who dwell in their world-renowned gardens in which giant plants have grown under the most improbable circumstances. Good spirits also inhabit their printing presses, stoves, enormous espresso equipment and an equally enormous dough machine. The machines and equipment are all given names and residents dwell upon effecting the energy of the machines in the same way that they meditate upon entering into the life of a plant. How often have you told a stalled automobile to "Please start up.." and sometimes had it respond to your request? Coincidence? Perhaps. Synchronicity? Could be.

There are physicists who admit that their theories were first experienced on a mystical level of consciousness and believe that the material objects which surround us are not passive and inert, but have their own vibrating dynamics. (Pythagoras told his followers that a stone is frozen music and that every object has its own personality.) Notable scientists have predicted that humankind will someday be able to harness the dynamics of unseen universal energies.

Some of the world's most renowned physicists believe that nothing is static in the universe. Instead, they believe that the universe is in a constant state of dynamic change since everything has a molecular structure of atoms that are constantly alive, vibrating and dancing. These beliefs relate to the realities of the fourth dimension that physicists and mystics seek. Presently, physicists are intrigued with the string theory that speculates that there are hundreds of dimensions beyond the known four in our universe. Some physicists also believe that there are universes beyond our own which elevates a discussion of religion among them. Some people are inclined to scoff at the belief that inanimate objects have a life of their own. Nevertheless, the belief continues to be acknowledged in innumerable everyday occurrences. At Northern Illinois University, a psychologist-educator requested his electricity lab students to relax and then told them to imagine being moving electrons inside of a hot wire, travelling through the wire's electrical coil while constantly coming into contact with other electrons. An instructor of a Chicago Cubs training program had his athletes stretch out on the floor. After a period of relaxation, he told them to "get into" the ball or bat and taste it, smell it, etc. On a different level, psychiatrists are using photographs to unlock psyches of patients by asking them to transport themselves into the meaning of a photograph in much the same way that the standard Rorschach test has been diagnostically employed to unlock the subconscious of the mind.

While vacationing on the Hawaiian island of Kauai, I had an experience similar to that of the colorful character, Don Juan in Carlos Castaneda's *Journey to Ixtlan*. In the book, Don Juan says that a sorcerer can focus on any object and find his way into and affect it. To prove it, Don Juan made a car inoperable by willfully "getting inside" the spark plugs. During my month's holiday on mystical Kauai, I rented a car and at the end of the rental period, I returned the car driving it to Lihue, the island's capitol. Lihue is about 21 miles away from the isolated cottage in which I stayed. The cottage is located at the end of Menehune Road near the entrance to the southern end of Waimea Canyon, often referred to as the Grand Canyon of the Pacific. After returning the car to Lihue, I had to hitchhike to Waimea since there was no public transportation on the island. I immediately got a ride from a teacher at a Kauai college who was able to take me to the Koloa intersection, about 15 miles from Waimea. It began to rain as I stood at the intersection, thumbing for a ride to Waimea. Hundreds of drivers ignored me during the hour I remained at the intersection. Finally, I started to walk towards Waimea, thumbing as I walked alongside the road—still being ignored by passing cars. Impulsively, I decided to test the power of the Projected Spatial Object Exercise by projecting energy into the brakes of the next car and willing the car to stop. I turned around and saw a red VW about 300 yards down the road. I gave myself to the moment, trusting that I might have the power to stop the VW. I concentrated on the vehicle and attempted to physically enter into the brakes with my consciousness. The VW stopped! The Kauaian native driver told me that the reason I had such bad luck at the Koloa intersection was because it is a favorite stopping place for Pele, the Hawaiian Goddess of Volcanoes, who travels through the islands and if she is in a temperamental mood, she can "do a number on you." I prefer to think that Pele desired to convince me that there are mystical forces on her garden island.

Actors in my workshop have also unleashed the kind of mystical experience I have had with the essence of the Projected Spatial Object Exercise. An actress practiced the exercise at home and projected her consciousness into a Melaleuca linariifolia tree (commonly known as the Flaxleaf Paperbark) in her garden. The tree thrives in harsh conditions and sends forth fluffy white flowers. The actress was indeed convinced she had entered into the tree's spirit for when she arose one February morning she beheld blooms on the tree, which she had never known to flower until the month of June.

I hope you can relate to the beauty of her experience. Maybe so, since we are becoming more receptive to the parapsychic experiences of people from all walks of life. It is known that Theravada Buddhists of Tibet feel consumed when concentrating upon an object. Visitors to museums in New York and Los Angeles were able to observe Tibetan monks recreate the 600 B.C. Kalachakra Mandala, using very fine grains of colored sand in an extremely meticulous procedure. It is conceivable that witnesses to this beautiful and sacred event were enlightened by the manner in which the disciple monks arrived at the center of their creation. Throughout the thirteen-day event, the monks inhabited a space of spiritual value as they made small deposits of colored grains of sand, a few at a time. Upon completion of their mandala, the sand was taken to a seashore where it was symbolically deposited in its ocean home. The Dalai Lama has described the mandala as "a vehicle for world peace." In western society, Jung envisioned mandalas in the rose windows of churches.

An actor should know how to inhabit another space and dissolve one's ego, with the same spirit of Tibetan monks, in order to inhabit the space of a character. The Projected Spatial Object Exercise dwells upon this desirable value.

THE PROJECTED SPATIAL OBJECT EXERCISE

Choice Suggestions of an animate or inanimate object.

Clock	Red cord
Screwdriver	Starfish
Vase with flower	Pliers
Indian headdress	Paperweight
Electric fan	Candlestick
Lonesome pine tree	Giant Rock
Ceramic bird	Incense burner
Box of nails	Burning candle
Kaleidoscope	Feather duster

Guidelines for the Projected Spatial Object Exercise

...Attempt to sense yourself entering into another dimension, as you transfer your consciousness to the interior of the object and capture the intrinsic nature which you imagine the object possesses. Endeavor to enter into the spirit of the object and charge it with your energy streams. Allow ego boundaries to dissolve as you become receptive to the object's essence, letting it absorb you so that you and the object are in conjunction.

...After getting to the very marrow of an object's nature, transport yourself beyond its spirit and mood. Create its form, textures and shape. Permit the object to become animated as you enter into its hidden dimensions. Tap into its energies. Give it commands as you pour energy waves into it and merge with it. Try to determine what it is about the object that causes internal and external changes.

Other Choices and Guidelines

Select a picture, painting or photograph which depicts numerous details of lines, shapes and forms. I offer actors a large collection of full-page magazine drawings and photographs (sans advertising copy) of bold pictorial subject matter. There are usually richer complexities in a picture or painting than in an object because of varying colors and other details.

...Inhabit the picture and let it come to life in the same manner as you did when using an object for the Projected Spatial Object Exercise. Experience the change of consciousness that results when you submerge yourself into a picture and sense it being alive and vibrating with motion. When his eyesight began to fade, French Impressionist painter Claude Monet projected himself into his beloved lily ponds which he then painted on huge canvases.

...An additional behavioral value can suddenly accrue from amidst the endless details. In experimenting with a possible behavioral choice for a character, be aware of the moments that have the precise value you are seeking. In a selection rich with behavioral possibilities, only certain experiential moments may offer you the specific qualities you wish.

...To fully realize your results in an improvisational or memorized scene, capture the intrinsic rhythm of the picture or painting as your imagination travels among the details. Establish the same rhythm in your walk, movements and gestures. Stanislavski said that an actor must find the rhythm of a character, cautioning that while a musician is given the rhythm by the composer's notes, an actor must search for the notes in the playwright's writing.

...Permit the picture or painting to affect you in such a way that you deeply feel its illuminating center. You can elevate the basic sensory place exercise to a much higher level by entering into your Projected Spatial Object and letting it take you to an unexperienced place of greater richness than places you have actually experienced. You never know what career momentum can occur by immersing yourself into the dramatic heart of pictorial matter. Sublime actress Jessica Lange was inspired to produce the movie *Country*, in which she also starred after she had been very moved by a newspaper photograph of a family being evicted from their farm. Her emotional involvement with the depicted event was so strong that she promoted the writing of the screenplay.

Often in my workshop, there are actors who have traveled one of many spiritual paths, as do many young people in search of some meaning amidst rampant materialism. A spiritually disciplined actress said that she did not have to think in this exercise as she permitted her choice "to think" for her. Another student said he experienced the higher consciousness that he had sought during twelve years of meditational practice but had never achieved. (However, I pointed out to him that perhaps his years of meditation had prepared him for his initial Projected Spatial Object Exercise.) The exercise gave him a heightened physical experience and awareness. Afterwards, he said, "In years of meditation, I never had a charge like that. It was like volts of electricity going through me." The picture he chose from my collection was of a space robot traveling through areas of cosmic forces. Coincidentally, within a short time, he was hired for an Academy Awards presentation to walk down the aisle as a robot.

Other Projected Spatial Object Exercises

Combine a picture or object with another choice(s).

EXAMPLE

To press my case
PSO - Yosemite cliff
IMO - Full moon in the head

To celebrate
PSO - Saguaro cactus
IMO - Caterpillar
OSO - Eyes, mouth, stomach

To bear witness to life's vitality
PSO - A Picasso cubist painting
Sp. Obj. - Traffic ticket
OSO - Arms

To question
PSO - Steering wheel
Sp. Obj. - Hand
IMO - Question mark
OSO - Forehead, eyes, hands

To make them shiver in their boots
PSO - Six shooter gun
IMO - Silver bullet

An interesting challenge is to create an introjection and attempt to project the introjection's psyche into an object, painting or picture.

BODY SEEING EXERCISE

This exercise enables you to grasp and inhabit your acting space in a different way as you contact movements, vibrations, people and objects by means of various parts of your body other than your eyes.

The following accounts illustrate concretely that this phenomenon is not only possible, but has been experienced by an interesting cross section of individuals.

Charles Lindbergh said that during his 1926 historical solo flight across the Atlantic—in a state of being both conscious and asleep—he could clearly see the fuselage behind him and his field of sight seemed limitless.

In Bombay, during experiments conducted by the Department of Parapsychology of the Government of India, blind people, following a period of meditation, were able to completely describe what they *"saw"* when their cheeks were placed against the lens of a microscope. This is parallel to the experience of deaf people who can hear music when a musical instrument is played while pressed against their bodies.

In Eugen Herrigel's *Zen in the Art of Archery,* the Master archer, while in darkness with his eyes closed, not only hit a target, but did so a second time—the second shot splintering the first arrow.

The preceding are among the events that inspired this exercise. They strongly underscore the belief that the human body is endowed with expressive areas too often taken for granted. And anything that the human body can experience is nourishment for an actor's choices, or ought to be.

The intention of this exercise is for you to explore the front, back and side parts of the body for their capacity to *"see."* In early sensory exercises you may have with your body's nerve endings, *"heard"* sound waves which registered on your spine or the back of your legs. Maria Callas, who greatly influenced public attitudes about art from the viewpoint of the true reality she experienced through her singing, spoke about having eyes in the back of her head. She was referring to career survival and the need to be acutely aware of those who would plunge a dagger in a rival's back. Having eyes in the back of one's head is not only requisite for career survival, but also can be an effective acting choice for capturing the mental state of a paranoid character.

As with other exercises in this book, I have, over a period of decades, observed substantial creative results from the Body Seeing Exercise when implemented in a scene. Among the results I have seen are:

- a greater command of one's acting space

- enhancement of the sensory network

- a greater centering and connection with other actors

- an unpredictable change in voice and speech

- a fresh physical presence

Guideline for the Body Seeing Exercise

...In your mind, picture your acting space. Maintain a sense of the command you have over the space that surrounds you by being able to "sense/see" it with your back, thighs, pelvis, knees, elbows or any other part of the body. With your imagination, create small or large camera lenses on various parts of your body.

...Focus on your targets and then interact with them.

...Explore a totally new way of grasping your environment. Immerse yourself into the visuals.

...Establish definite points of focus or viewpoints. Remember you can choose in what direction you "see" no matter where the body part is, e.g., the front of the chest can see behind you if you wish it.

...Feel free to lose focal points when moving on to other focal points.

...Move your focal points. For example, let those in back of you revolve to the front, so that if you "see" a chair behind you, move the focal point so that the chair is now in front of you.

EXAMPLES OF THE BODY SEEING EXERCISE

Action	Choices
To inspire	Forehead, chest, knees, end of toes
To agonize for love	Belly and groin

Action	Choices
To seek freedom	Arms and legs as periscopes
To make myself alluring	Breasts to see erotic parts
To speak the unspeakable	Palms, soles of feet, nape of neck
To win my place	Breasts and feet as eyes of Buddha
To assimilate everything	Skin to see vibrations
To share my space	Kneecaps as two large eyeballs
To see the horror	Camera moving inside the body Eyes with X-ray vision
To stay on top	Fingertips, hair, nostrils
To spread the word	Top of head, vocal cords, nails

BODY SEEING
COMBINATION EXAMPLES

To con everyone
Body Seeing - Breasts and butt
Introjection

To find happiness
Body Seeing - The entire body
Sp. Obj. - Child singing and playing marimbas
Ch. Imp. - Tranquil
   OA: Night air in nose
   DA: - Base of brain and into entire body

To leap into darkness
Body Seeing - Third eye
DSO - The sea

To understand the unthinkable
Body Seeing - Palm of right hand
P&P - Chin: to hold the world responsible

To consciously direct God's love
Body Seeing - Camera lens as Third eye
            Both palms and thighs
OSO - Navel, heart, cheeks

DISTANT SPATIAL OBJECT

Have you ever heard of the phenomenon known as remote viewing—a skill by which a person can perceive and describe objects, persons or events that are removed by time or place, or both? If you accept the possibility of remote viewing then you believe that part of your consciousness is able to depart from you and return.

There are scientists who claim to have discovered radio waves coming from over a hundred different galaxies (our earth is part of just one galaxy). Other scientists talk about the eventual use of universal forces for many of our human needs. Researchers in many fields are exploring the ways in which our minds are capable of reaching beyond the parameters of our bodies. We observe this in nature when birds, with their ability to contact magnetic atmospheric forces, know the precise time of the year and the precise direction to migrate.

At one time, seized with apprehension that the Soviet Union was ahead of the United States in parapsychology, the Central Intelligence Agency hired psychics to determine if there was any plutonium in North Korea. Psychics were also consulted about the fate and treatment of American hostages during the Iran crisis of 1979.

Avid television viewers of programs that examine either parapsychology or real-life crime mysteries are acquainted with remote viewing psychics, working in conjunction with law enforcement agencies, to locate missing persons. Additionally, there are even health maintenance organizations plans that have developed an interest in employing remote healers who are reputed to have healed people many miles away. Experiments by these HMOs suggests that patients who were subjected to the healing energy of a remote healer actually felt better in less than an hour. An experiment in which healing thoughts and concerned thoughts, along with prayer, were projected towards four hundred people revealed that they got better, if not completely healed. The results of this experiment argue that many of us who are not considered to be full-fledged psychics are, nevertheless, capable of remote healing and reaching beyond the parameters of our bodies.

Since the time of the ancient Greeks, people have been fascinated with the uncanny ability of the mind and soul to travel to distant places. There have been numerous such reports of civilians, during times of war, who had been in contact with loved ones wounded or dying in battle thousands of miles away. Many firmly believed that a universal force played an active role in these out-of-body contacts.

So, what has this to do with an acting choice? This exercise would not be in this book if I had not repeatedly witnessed sufficient results in the use of it, thereby making it valid for those who are creatively fascinated by its potential. This exercise is designed to expand the acting space you inhabit for a character, while giving your actual space more tactile sensations. You can develop a new and more imaginative perception of your acting space as you transport yourself to a distant place and then send its tactile nature to your actual acting space.

Guidelines to the Distant Spatial Object Exercise

...A certain kind of zeal and strong personal desire are needed in exploring this exercise. Permit it to be a reflection of your creative spirit to go beyond ordinary boundaries.

...Foremost in the exercise, you should be involved in contacting the tactile energy of a distant place you have been to before. It can be nearby, a few miles away or halfway across the world, but it should be a place to which you have actually been, and the contents of which remain vivid in your emotional memory. Project your energy to your chosen place and immerse yourself into it. Sense your place all around you— above you, beneath you and at your sides—until you are able to draw from those sensations to create the *behavioral* experience you seek while bringing the place close to you so that you can feel a personal contact with it.

...After you see, smell, hear and taste the place around you, immerse yourself into the textures of the experiences using only the texture experience appropriate for your performance space.

...Keep all of your senses alert as you transfer your mind to your distant space. With the entire scope of your imagination and the sensitivity of your nerve endings, sense the magnetic energy of the event.

...Upon arriving at your chosen place, explore

the tactile ingredients and permit them to create the physical behavior desired for your character's action.

...As you contact the personal essence of your choice, do not feel that you are limited to the parameters of only your body parts. Rather, also acknowledge the changes in your biochemistry, such as changes in the levels of your endorphins and adrenaline and their consequent effects.

...Reach down into the deepest sources of your consciousness to sense the "nervous system" of the earth and transfer that tactile distant experience into your own nervous system. Then, let your body creatively manifest the experience.

EXAMPLES

Action	Distant Spatial Object
To show my power	Hawaiian Mauna Loa Volcano
To try to look at the bright side	Japanese spa
To bear out the impeachment call	Middle of Death Valley
To inflame their hearts	Garden of billowing flowers
To bounce back and forth	Ramshackle bar in Cleveland
To celebrate life	Woods in Connecticut
To captivate people	Daigohonzon object in Mt. Fuji temple
To go back in time	Agamemnon's Tomb in Mycenae
To swagger	Cowboy movie set
To share the loss	Deforested area

Action	Distant Spatial Object
To quiet the storm	Canadian Rocky Mountains
To disconnect	A hometown street
To bluff my way	Three ring circus
To guard	Cement barriers on island of Crete constructed to stop Nazi boats
To evaluate the situation	Sea of grass
To connect	Rock Island in Atlantic Ocean near Salem
To possess	A Tijuana hotel
To reminisce	Interior of a house in Brooklyn, N.Y.
To find the humor in the pain	Giant chicken farm
To find the flow	A courthouse in Santa Paula, CA
To find my bearings	Father's coffin
To tantalize	Tropical Hawaiian beach
To reach my center	Esalen Hot Springs
To shut out the nightmare	Berlin Wall
To try to find an answer	Auschwitz
To make a place for myself	Water tower in Ohio
To map uncharted territory	Grand Canyon

Distant Spatial Object Combination

EXAMPLES

To keep my center
DSO - Golden Gate Bridge
OSO - Hands
Ch. Imp. - Determination
    OA: Electric current in head
    DA: Hand

To get all I can
DSO - Doughnut shop
IMO - Grasshoppers from abdomen to shoulders

To impale
DSO - Racing herd of gazelles
IMO - Neon in veins and extremities

To open up
DSO - A place in Detroit
PSO - *Psychology Today* magazine

To get rid of someone
DSO - Pyramids of Egypt
IMO - A hand
P&P - Ears to hear dissonant sounds
    Nose to alternately smell good and bad
    Thighs and upper arms to embrace and repel

To fight panic
DSO - Childhood bedroom
Aura - Red eyes

To chill the blood
DSO - Smoldering volcano
IMO - Poisonous snakes inside arms
      Steel bars in legs and torso
OSO - Eyes and genitals

To utter the unspoken
DSO - Jasmine porch
P&P - Feet to step out of the crowd
Ch. Imp. - Delirious
      OA: Chanting in ears
      DA: Extremities

To drift in time and space
DSO - Monterey Bay
IMO - Lover's heart in head and upper chest

To sell it hard
DSO - University City Walk
OSO - People

To bluff my way
DSO - Traffic intersection in Rome
Sp. Obj. - Sound waves of Beethoven's Ninth

Although your choice of a Distant Spatial Object should be limited to a place to which you have actually been, as mentioned earlier, it is conceivable that you can select a time-specific place to which to travel with your imagination. Denzel Washington, who received an Academy Award and a Golden Globe Award for his role in the Civil War film *Glory*, had a scene which called for his character to be whipped. He prepared for it by kneeling and getting into the essence and spirit of black men who had gone through that kind of experience in the past.

EXAMPLES OF IMAGINED DISTANT SPATIAL OBJECT IN THE PAST

Custer's Last Stand

Man's first landing on the moon

Jerusalem during the Crusades

An underground shelter during a WWII bombing of London

A July 4th celebration in New York City in 1876

A theater event in ancient Greece

OTHER DISTANT PLACES TO WHICH TO TRAVEL USING YOUR IMAGINATION

Earth's Magnetic Field

The Sun

The Milky Way

The Moon

Prehistoric Fertility Goddess in Space

Den of the Underworld

Fiery Core of the Earth

The North Star

HIGHLIGHT EXERCISE

You have to upset yourself. Unless you do, you cannot act. And there comes a time in one's life when you don't want to do it anymore. You know a scene is coming where you'll have to cry and scream and all those things, and it's always bothering you, always eating away at you...and you can't just walk through it...it would be really disrespectful not to try to do your best.

Marlon Brando

The Highlight Exercise examines the versatility of your power to control conflicting emotions even as you ascend to the highest emotional plateaus. This exercise will give you enormous creative control when you take yourself to the very edge of intense feelings. In that respect, the exercise is related to the birth of the Stanislavski System which is based in part on Stanislavski's study of great international actors who displayed perfect control when they performed at their peak powers.

It is important that you abandon yourself to this exercise without hesitation nor shying away from its extremes. You may think that you are being a "ham," but "hamming it up" can be a winning feature. There are top performers who have invested considerable time and energy to refine and endow their "ham" impulses with extraordinary dramatic power.

A most impressive feature in an actor's talent is the emotional strength tapped during a scene which requires combustible behavior. A powerful acting instrument possesses the skill and creativity to achieve high states of emotion through behavior, capturing images and feelings that burn into the memory of an audience.

Intense emotions must be convincing for otherwise they can seem bombastic or semi-faked. Only a well-trained talent can be used to its full capacity to take emotional moments to the very edge.

This exercise is intended to give you keener insight into the vast resources of your emotional equipment. It offers a way to abandon yourself as you connect with deeper layers of your nerves and sinews; to shift your emotions into high gear and stretch beyond your previous limits without being hesitant or afraid; to test your commitment to acting through your willingness to go over the top.

Our day-to-day existence does not require us, moment to moment, to be fully aware of all the facets of our true essence. However, in acting, you cannot completely know a character unless you have explored all sides of that character. This exercise requires you to pinpoint the polarities of a character and maintain a counteraction between them. For example, feeling an element of trust in the midst of suspicion; maintaining a spark of hope during a time of fear; being elated about winning a coveted role yet having sympathy for the misery of a friend who lost out; or maintaining high moral and ethical values in public while abusing one's family members in private.

Initially, with this exercise, you may elect to work with a single emotion, but keep in mind we can experience life with mixed emotions, even when a passionate emotion seemingly rules. The emotion your character encounters in a scene can be made complex by underlying feelings quite opposite to the dominant emotion. This exercise can help you to pinpoint the psychology of contradictory feelings. The amalgamation of different values will add dimension to your character's behavior. It will capture that strange yet common experience of suddenly feeling an incongruous emotion in the midst of an overwhelming primary emotion.

In the 19th century, Francois Delsarte taught acting and singing. He began as a singer, but faulty training botched his voice. Unfortunately, he turned to discovering principles of dramatic expression which in turn damaged the evolution of modern acting. Well-known actors studied with Delsarte and thereby helped to promulgate his superficial theories. He devised a series of postures and mannerisms, which imitated the external manifestation of emotion and which he believed reflected universal reactions to various stimuli. By doing so, he fostered a popular approach to enacting an emotion in a regimented way. As we know, Stanislavski rebelled against this cookie-cutter view of acting.

Carl Jung postulated that we experience the world in four ways: sensation, thinking, feeling and intuition. Though Jung thought it was possible to classify people into one of these types, he acknowledged that we each have the capacity to experience life in any or all of these ways. This capacity leads to the contradictions in a character which give a role its humanity and its inner state of flux. Opposing psychological values add rich dimensions to a role.

The ability to create a highly emotional moment, or to sustain a powerful behavioral state, is frequently the determining factor in casting. A director will often select the most challenging moment in a role to decide if an actor will be able to handle the challenge with conviction and imagination. When confronted with such a casting situation, or in giving an actual performance, the actor must know how much energy to use. Too much energy can mar an audition, reading, or performance. In this exercise, you will experiment to determine the amount of energy you need for powerful moments.

In a workshop situation, try not to be concerned with being obvious or going overboard with the exercise. If you have never worked with extreme emotional moments, you will correct that deficiency and discover your ability to push yourself to higher emotional limits.

Guidelines for the Highlight Exercise and Emotion Groups

1. Select an action. Your action should suggest a mixture of emotions, not just one emotion.

2. Select one emotion choice from two or three Highlight Exercise emotions groups. Each emotion group comprises a range of related emotional experience. The range permits you the opportunity to hone in on and select a precise emotion. For example, in emotional group #11, you might select the emotional experience of Respectfulness as a stronger choice than Trust.

EMOTION GROUPS

1. JOYOUS
    TRIUMPHANT
    BLISSFULNESS
    CONTENTMENT
    HOPEFUL
    TRANQUIL
    STUDIED CONTROL

2. DISGUST
    DISTASTEFUL
    TURNED-OFF
    UPTIGHT
    ANNOYANCE
    EMBARRASSMENT
    IRRITATION
    RESTLESSNESS

3. TURNED-ON
   UNCONTROLLABLE LAUGHTER
   ORGASM
   DRUNK
   HIGH ELATION
   HORNY
   VOLUPTUOUSNESS
   SENSUAL

4. PAIN
   MENTAL SUFFERING
   HUMILIATION
   HIGH-STRUNG
   INSENSIBLE STUPOR
   DISBELIEF
   CONFUSED

5. SUSPICIOUS
   HIGHLY CAUTIOUS
   CURIOSITY

6. SORROW
   BROKEN-HEARTED
   DISAPPOINTMENT
   LAMENT
   REPENTANT
   DESPONDENT
   HOPELESSNESS
   SUPPLICATION
   FRUSTRATION

7. VINDICTIVENESS
   ANGER
   MURDEROUS RAGE
   HOSTILITY
   BITTERNESS
   SPITEFULNESS
   CRUELTY
   OUTSPOKEN
   SUPERIORITY
   SARCASTIC

8. WEAKNESS
   FATIGUE
   WEARISOME
   SUBMISSION
   RELIEF

9. WORRY
   FEAR
   PANIC
   ANXIOUS
   COWARDICE
   SHY
   FRANTIC

10. HATE
    UNCONCERN
    REPULSIVENESS
    ILL-MANNERED
    INDIFFERENCE

11. TRUST
    SYMPATHETIC
    GIVING
    CONCERN
    GRATEFULNESS
    RESPECTFULNESS
    REVERENCE

12. SUFFOCATION
    STARVATION
    EXTREME THIRST
    SUNSTROKE
    HEART ATTACK
    NERVOUS
    BREAKDOWN
    AMNESIA
    SHELL SHOCK
    CLAUSTROPHOBIA
    BREATHLESSNESS

13. SEXUAL LONGING
    SEXUAL FRUSTRATION
    AFFECTION
    ATTRACTION
    LONELINESS
    REJECTION
    INFERIORITY FEELINGS

...It will require the best of your sensitivity and imagination to trigger what may seem like functioning in a different dimension of creative reality. Your reward may be a sense of being completely separated from your usual self as you create the smoldering energies of a character's complex psyche. It can be the ultimate experience of losing yourself in a character.

...Permit one of your Highlight choices to suddenly come into focus while other choices suddenly disappear, only to reemerge later.

...Enjoy the aesthetics of the experience.

...Permit your sensitivity to trigger the Highlight experience.

...The exercise is not linear. When you are working with two or more emotions, do not create the first emotion and then discontinue it when you add the second or third emotion. One choice builds upon another. Their merging renders different values at different moments.

...It is important that you gauge the relative levels of energy you put into emotional selections. Since all of your selections are relevant to your results, do not permit one emotion to be victorious over another; instead, maintain an interplay between them.

...Permit the emotional choices to bristle with colors. Think of paintings or even clothing fabrics with wildly divergent colors.

...Try to develop a sense of riding a peak emotional moment with ease. Like any demanding undertaking, this exercise will get your adrenaline flowing and may lead to a feeling of fulfillment.

...Sometimes in the middle of a Highlight you may sound one note that can have a shattering effect on an audience. Eric Clapton relates that he wishes to be able to make an audience cry on a single note. In the middle of a musical number, he seeks that moment when he can create a single sound that will make his audience "quiver with emotion." I'm sure that you can recall performances wherein the entire spectrum of an actor's craft suddenly clicked into place and you were carried away by a heart-rending or hair-raising or uproarious moment.

EXAMPLES

To assert myself
Panic: IMO - Tarantula in head
　　　IMO - Invading virus in body
Extreme concern: Ch. Imp.
　　　　　　　　OA: Energetic white light
　　　　　　　　　　　in stomach
　　　　　　　DA: Head

To put myself on the line
Repulsive: Stimulus of skin crawling
Spitefulness: Sp. Obj. - Spiders

To avoid the issue
Optimism: Aura - Blue from top of the head
Dread: Ch. Imp.
　　　OA: Queasy stomach
　　　DA: Eyes

To protect a friend
Sympathy: Aura - Lavender in legs
                 Green - Rest of the body
Hostility: OSO - Teeth
Anxiety: Introjection

To be the life of the party
Outspoken: Introjection
          Ch. Imp.
            OA: Arrows in chest
            DA: Sinus
Narcissistic: Sp. Obj. - Video screens
Affectionate: Aura - Yellow
               P&P - Thighs to hustle
               Body alive with telling details

To stop the ugly rumors, now
Suspicious: Place - Visual
Extreme Anger: Hot fire in gut
                  Sound of war drums
Trust: OSO - Hands
           Thighs

To gross them out
Uncontrollable laughter: Sp. Obj. - Hands
Outspoken: Introjection

To ventilate the problem
Jealousy: P&P - Hands to grab what's mine
                Eyes to see things the way
                I want them to be
Anger: Aura - Red in the eyes
        IMO - Hot spike

To get ready to do battle
Organized: OSO - Eyes
Nervous stimulation: Ch. Imp.
                         OA: Electric current in feet
                         DA: Stomach

To win at any cost
Uncontrollable Laughter: Ch. Imp.
                         OA: Electricity in feet
                         DA: Entire body
Suspicious: IMO - Chess set in head
                  Bees in bloodstream
Hate: OSO - Stomach
        Sp. Obj. - Diamonds

To seek the truth
Disgust: Aura - Red
Restlessness: Ch. Imp.
                  OA: Ice water in feet
                  DA: Head
                  Introjection

Appendix

ACTION LIST

To Admire the World

To Admit Past Mistakes

To Advise

To Annihilate the Tyrants

To Argue the Point

To Arrive at the Last Stop

To Assault

To Attract and Possess All I Desire

To Avoid

To Avoid Being Tracked Down

To Avoid Conversation

To Avoid Delicate Matters

To Avoid Doing the Inevitable

To Avoid the Issue

To Avoid the Truth

To Awaken

To Bait

To Beat Down

To Blast

To Bluff My Way

To Bolster Up

To Bomb Them with My Power

To Break Loose

To Break Through

To Break Out of My Shell

To Break the Balance

To Bring Out the Corrupt Nature

To Bring Them to Their Knees

To Brighten the Atmosphere

To Bruise

To Brush Over Delicate Matters

To Burn All My Bridges

To Burst Forward

To Bury My Problems

To Call the Next Move

To Captivate

To Captivate People

To Captivate Their Imagination

To Capture the Moment

To Carry Out an Important Mission

To Cast Off Mediocrity

To Cast Off the Yoke

To Cast Out the Devil

To Catch the Eye

To Change Directions

To Change the Mood

To Change their Minds

To Chew Up and Spit Out

To Claim My Position

To Clearly Explain My Anger

To Climb Out of Myself

To Cling

To Cool Things Off

To Come into My Own

To Come Out on Top

To Complain

To Complain Like Hell

To Complete an Important Mission

To Con Everyone

To Confront the Fear and Let Go

To Confuse Everything

To Connect Everything

To Connect to My Dream

To Connect with the World

To Conquer Evil

To Contain My Moments

To Control People

To Cool Them Off

To Cover Up My Guilt

To Cut the Crap

To Cut Through the Fog

To Defend What is Mine

To Delve into My Fantasies

To Demand Recognition

To Demand Their Best

To Deny I Have a Problem

To Derail

To Destroy

To Devastate My Surroundings

To Devour

To Dictate the Law

To Discover a New Way

To Dive into the Wreck

To Discover the Humor of It

To Discover the Truth

To Do It With Spirit

To Do My Work

To Do the Inevitable

To Do What I Have to Do

To Dominate Everything

To Draw from the Roots

To Draw the Line

To Dump On

To Embrace the Epiphany

To Encourage Everyone to Love the World

To Enforce My Will

To Enlighten

To Escape into Another World

To Evade the Issue

To Examine My Folly

To Excite Someone

To Explain My Circumstances

To Explain Where I'm Coming From

To Exploit My Status

To Explore in Detail

To Expose the S.O.B.

To Express my Needs

To Face Up To

To Fight Back

To Fight for What I Believe In

To Fight the Lie

To Figure Out

To Find a Place for Myself

To Find an Easy Way Out

To Find Magic

To Find My Bearings

To Find Out

To Find Protection

To Find Something to Do

To Find the Answer

To Find the Dividing Line

To Find the Father in Me

To Find the Mother in Me

To Find the Truth

To Fit In

To Flow with the Tide

To Flush Them Out

To Fly into the Wind

To Fly the Coop

To Follow

To Follow My Star

To Force Connection

To Form a Bond with Those Around Me

To Free Myself

To Freeze the Blood

To Get All I Can

To Get Along

To Get Away from People

To Get Back on Course

To Get Back to a Better Time

To Get in Bed

To Get in Everywhere

To Get It All Out

To Get Lost in My Sexual Fantasies

To Get Next To

To Get Off the Hot Seat

To Get On the Good Side

To Get Out of Myself

To Get Rid of Someone

To Get Some Food

To Get the Job Done

To Get the Upper Hand

To Get Their Attention

To Get Them Off My Back

To Get Them to Look On the Bright Side

To Get Things in Focus

To Get to the Heart of the Matter

To Get to the Point

To Get Under Their Skin

To Give All the Love I Have

To Give My Power Away

To Give Myself

To Go Against the Grain

To Go All the Way

To Go Back in Time

To Go For It

To Go Off into My Own World

To Go One Step Further

To Go Where No Man Has Gone Before

To Go With the Flow

To Grope for Words

To Grope in the Dark

To Gross Them Out

To Guide

To Harbor a Grudge

To Haul Over the Coals

To Heal

To Hear the Results

To Hit the Bull's-eye

To Hit Where It Hurts

To Hold Fast to Tradition

To Hold Myself Together

To Hold On to Someone

To Hold On to My Bearings

To Hold Their Interest

To Hold Up

To Hustle a Fast One

To Incite

To Include Another

To Induce

To Inflame

To Inflame Your Brain

To Instigate

To Intimidate

To Investigate

To Invite

To Involve Myself in Their Secret Lives

To Involve Them in My Experience

To Inspire

To Cunningly Justify My Outrage

To Joke with Them

To Jump at the Chance

To Jump In

To Keep a Safe Distance

To Keep an Open Mind

To Keep Attached to People

To Keep Everything

To Keep from Ripping Out Their Guts

To Keep from Being Destroyed

To Keep from Sinking

To Keep Going

To Keep Going for the Love of It

To Keep in Touch with People

To Keep Myself Attached to People

To Keep Out of Trouble

To Keep the Lid On

To Keep the Situation in Hand

To Keep Them Unbalanced

To Keep Things Going My Way

To Know My Power

To Know When Enough Is Enough

To Lay My Ass on the Line

To Lead by the Nose

To Leap into a Trap

To Leap onto the Bull

To Learn How to Connect

To Leave My Old Self Behind

To Lend Myself to the Situation

To Let It Out

To Level

To Liberate the Oppressed

To Lift Their Spirits

To Listen

To Live It Up

To Live Moment to Moment

To Look into Someone's Soul

To Look on the Bright Side of Life

To Look Out for Number One

To Lust

To Maintain My Balance

To Make Amends

To Make Bold My Point of View

To Make People Do What I Want Them to Do

To Make a Place for Myself

To Make a Simple Connection

To Make a Sleazy Deal

To Make a Stand

To Make the Atmosphere Crackle

To Make the Day Mine

To Make Them Acknowledge My Presence

To Make Them Hunger for More

To Make Them See It My Way

To Make Them Sorry They Were Ever Born

To Make Them Understand

To Make Things Comfortable

To Map Uncharted Territory

To Master the Possibilities

To Meet My God's Vengeance

To Merge My Soul With the Universe

To Mock Everyone

To Mold

To Move from the Center

To Nail

To Needle

To Not Give Up

To Nurture Those Around Me

To Observe Everything

To Open the Pandora's Box

To Own This Place

To Pay Them Back

To Penetrate the Core of Evil

To Pester

To Pick Up the Pieces

Th Pierce the Universe

To Piss Them Off

To Plant a Seed of Doubt

To Play With Them

To Plead My Case

To Please

To Plow Through the Blizzard

To Possess Everything

To Practice Like a Child

To Prepare Myself for Love

To Prepare to Pounce

To Prevail

To Probe More Deeply

To Protect a Friend

To Protect Myself

To Provoke

To Pry Some Confidential Information

To Pull Strings

To Pursue an Attraction

To Push My Case

To Push the Agenda

To Push Their Buttons

To Put a Jewel in Your Crown

To Put Them on the Spot

To Put on Ice

To Put the World in Order

To Put to Proof

To Quell Their Anxiety

To Question Everything

To Quiet

To Raise Hell

To Ram It Home Unflinchingly

To Reach My Center

To Realize a Dream

To Realize the Buddha in Myself

To Rebel Against

To Refuse

To Relish the Moment

To Regain My Confidence

To Remain in the Limelight

To Remind

To Remove Myself from the Situation

To Resist

To Respond

To Respond to the Call of Life

To Retain a Sense of Myself

To Reveal Myself

To Rip Somebody's Guts Out

To Rise Above My Anger

To Rouse

To Rule with Power

To Rule the Roost

To Save My Soul

To Save Myself

To Save the World

To Scar

To Schmooze with Panache

To Seduce

To See All Viewpoints

To See It Through to the End

To See Nowhere to Go

To See the Horror

To See What I Can Get

To See the World Through a Child's Eyes

To See Through the Fog

To Seek Comfort

To Seek Greener Pastures

To Seek Hidden Treasure

To Seek Romance

To Seize an Opportunity

To Sell a Bill of Goods

To Sell Crap

To Sell My Vision

To Send Them to Hell

To Set on Fire

To Settle in a Dream

To Shape

To Share My Space

To Show My True Colors

To Show Who's the Boss

To Shut Out the World

To Shut Out the Nightmare

To Skirt the Issue

To Smash

To Sneak Through the Back Door

To Soak Up Everything

To Solve a Problem

To Soothe the Pain

To Spell Out My Priorities

To Spew Philosophic Rhetoric

To Spin My Web

To Spiritually Lead

To Spoil the Party

To Spring the Trap

To Squirm Through

To Stab

To Stand My Ground

To State My Intentions

To Stay Where I Am

To Stir

To Stir Up the Moment

To Stop This

To Stop Them in Their Tracks

To Straighten Them Out

To Swim Against

To Take a Chance

To Take Care Of

To Take Charge of Today

To Take in Hand

To Take Them Down With Me

To Tantalize

To Tear Back to the Raw Elements

To Tease

To Tell It Like It Is

To Tell the Whole Truth

To Think Big

To Throw Off the Rails

To Throw It All To the Wind

To Tower Over

To Toy With Them

To Trap My Prey

To Try to Do Something

To Try to Find an Answer

To Try to Hit the Target

To Understand the Unthinkable

To Undermine

To Unmask the Face of Deception

To Urge

To Wait It Out

To Weaken Their Defenses

To Win at Any Cost

To Win Someone Over

To Wish the World Well

PERMISSION TO REPRINT ACKNOWLEDGMENT

The author wishes to thank the following for permission to reprint selections in the book. The author apologizes if there are any inadvertent omissions which will be, upon notification, corrected in future editions. The first column of numbers indicates page numbers in the text.

Introjection Chapter

P. 79   "The Grandfather of all Cool Actors Becomes the Godfather" 3/10/73
(c)1973 Time Inc. Reprinted by permission.

P. 79   "I Cannot Possibly Make Hitler Sympathetic."
Copyright (c) 1972
by the New York Times Co.
Reprinted by permission.

Physiological and Psychological Chapter

P. 110 "Oscar Ichazo and the Arica Institute."
(A conversation between Oscar Ichazo and Sam Keen.)
Reprinted by Permission from
Psychology Today, Copyright(c)1973
(Sussex Publishers, Inc.)

Highlight Chapter

P. 156 "The Grandfather of all Cool Actors Becomes the Godfather" 3/10/73
(c)1973 Time Inc. Reprinted by permission.

NOTES

NOTES

NOTES